THE REASONABLE ROBOT

AI and people do not compete on a level-playing field. Self-driving vehicles may be safer than human drivers, but laws often penalize such technology. People may provide superior customer service, but businesses are automating to reduce their taxes. AI may innovate more effectively, but an antiquated legal framework constrains inventive AI. In *The Reasonable Robot*, Ryan Abbott argues that the law should not discriminate between AI and human behavior and proposes a new legal principle that will ultimately improve human well-being. This work should be read by anyone interested in the rapidly evolving relationship between AI and the law.

Ryan Abbott, MD, JD, MTOM, PhD, is Professor of Law and Health Sciences at the School of Law, University of Surrey, and Adjunct Assistant Professor of Medicine at UCLA. A physician and patent attorney, Abbott's research on law and technology has helped shape the international dialogue on these topics. He has served as an expert for the World Health Organization, the World Intellectual Property Organization, the European Commission, and the Parliament of the United Kingdom. Abbott also spearheaded the first patent applications to disclose inventions made autonomously by an AI. In 2019, he was named one of the 50 most influential people in Intellectual Property by *Managing IP* magazine.

The Reasonable Robot

ARTIFICIAL INTELLIGENCE AND THE LAW

RYAN ABBOTT

University of Surrey School of Law

CAMBRIDGE
UNIVERSITY PRESS

University Printing House, Cambridge CB2 8BS, United Kingdom

One Liberty Plaza, 20th Floor, New York, NY 10006, USA

477 Williamstown Road, Port Melbourne, VIC 3207, Australia

314–321, 3rd Floor, Plot 3, Splendor Forum, Jasola District Centre, New Delhi – 110025, India

79 Anson Road, #06–04/06, Singapore 079906

Cambridge University Press is part of the University of Cambridge.

It furthers the University's mission by disseminating knowledge in the pursuit of education, learning, and research at the highest international levels of excellence.

www.cambridge.org
Information on this title: www.cambridge.org/9781108472128
DOI: 10.1017/9781108631761

First published 2020

A catalogue record for this publication is available from the British Library.

Library of Congress Cataloging-in-Publication Data
NAMES: Abbott, Ryan, author.
TITLE: The reasonable robot : Artificial Intelligence and the law / Ryan Abbott, University of Surrey School of Law.
DESCRIPTION: Cambridge, United Kingdom ; New York, NY, USA : Cambridge University Press, 2020. | Includes index.
IDENTIFIERS: LCCN 2019042234 | ISBN 9781108472128 (hardback) | ISBN 9781108459020 (ebook)
SUBJECTS: LCSH: Artificial intelligence – Law and legislation. | Personality (Law)
CLASSIFICATION: LCC K564.C6 .A23 2020 | DDC 343.09/99–dc23
LC record available at https://lccn.loc.gov/2019042234

ISBN 978-1-108-47212-8 Hardback
ISBN 978-1-108-45902-0 Paperback

To my Mother

Contents

Introduction: Artificial Intelligence and the Law

The rise of powerful AI will be either the best or the worst thing ever to happen to humanity. We don't yet know which.

– Stephen Hawking

Artificial intelligence (AI) is doing more than ever before, and often doing it cheaper, faster, and better than people are. In 2017, the company DeepMind developed an AI, AlphaGo Master, that beat the world champion of the board game Go. Many experts had predicted AI's Go dominance would take another decade given the game's complexity. There are more possible board configurations in Go than there are atoms in the universe. Later in 2017, a revised version of AlphaGo, AlphaGo Zero, beat AlphaGo Master one hundred games to zero. It did this after training for just three days by playing against itself. Unlike its predecessors, AlphaGo Zero never learned from human examples.

Go was the last traditional board game at which people could outperform machines. There is now an entire field of activity at which AI dramatically surpasses people. While AlphaGo's victory was an exciting technical landmark, it has had limited social impact because playing board games is not the most practical endeavor. But they are one of the oldest measures of machine intelligence, and AI's ascendency hints that it may soon automate a broader range of tasks, perhaps sooner than many anticipate, and it may do so in spectacular fashion.

Alphabet, which owns DeepMind, is not investing in AI to dominate the field for competitive board games. In principle, if an AI can be trained to recognize patterns in Go, then it can be trained to recognize pneumonia in an X-ray or pedestrians on a road. Indeed, DeepMind is already being applied to solve practical challenges. In 2018, DeepMind's AI AlphaFold outperformed all of its ninety-eight competitors in a challenge aimed at predicting the three-dimensional structure of proteins – a task critical to drug discovery. Unlike playing Go, predicting protein folding is an important, common, and real-life scientific problem. Similarly, again in 2018, researchers found that another DeepMind AI correctly referred patients with more than fifty distinct eye diseases for specialist care in 94 percent of cases, matching the performance of expert clinicians. In 2019, DeepMind AI was able to consistently predict development of acute kidney failure forty-eight hours earlier than human physicians, which could ultimately prevent around 30 percent of cases from ever occurring.

The future social impact of these advances will be tremendous. Already, impressive-sounding era titles such as the Fourth Industrial Revolution, the Second Machine Age, and the Automation Revolution are being used to describe the coming disruption. Among other things, AI is predicted to generate a massive amount of wealth by changing the future of work. This has long been the experience with AI's automating physical work, such as in automobile manufacturing, but AI is now moving into automating mental work, and not only relatively simple service activities like operating a cash register at McDonald's. AI is completing tasks performed by doctors, lawyers, and scientists.

IBM's flagship AI Watson, which famously won a game of *Jeopardy!* in 2011, works in a range of fields. In health care, Watson (now a brand comprised of a variety of AI systems) analyzes the genetics of cancer patients to help select appropriate drug treatments, a task that a group of human experts can also do but which remains a complex and demanding activity. For some patients, it can require around 160 collective work hours by a team of highly trained health care providers. By contrast, a 2017 study reports that Watson can outperform the standard practice and that it only requires about 10 minutes to do so,[1] although Watson's performance has proven controversial.[2]

Several companies claim their AI can already outdo human doctors in certain areas of medical practice. This is not surprising. Machines are able to memorize every bit of medical literature ever created and process practice experience from countless human lifetimes. Plus, they never need a rest break. In 2017, a Chinese company reported its robot Xiao Yi took and passed, by a wide margin, the National Medical Licensing Examination, the test required to become a medical doctor in China. Xiao Yi knows the contents of dozens of medical textbooks, millions of medical records, and hundreds of thousands of articles, but to pass the test it also had to learn, reason, and make judgments by itself. Researchers at IBM have even reported that Watson quietly passed the equivalent exam in the United States after being prohibited from formally taking it.

Of course, just passing tests does not make someone, or something, a doctor. Once AI is consistently better than a doctor at diagnosing certain diseases, managing prescriptions, or performing surgeries, AI is still unlikely to completely automate medical care. But these developments suggest that there are already aspects of medical care susceptible to automation, and that fewer doctors will be needed once there are more efficient doctors augmented by AI.

1 AI LEGAL NEUTRALITY

The law plays a critical role in the use and development of AI. Laws establish binding rules and standards of behavior to ensure social well-being and protect individual rights, and they can help us realize the benefits of AI while minimizing its risks – which are significant. AI has been involved in flash crashes in the stock market, cybercrime, and social and political manipulation. Famous technologists like Elon Musk and academics like Stephen Hawking have even argued that AI may doom the human race. Most concerns, however, focus on nearer-term and more practical problems such as technological unemployment, discrimination, and safety.

Although the risks and benefits of AI are widely acknowledged, there is little consensus about how best to regulate AI and jurisdictions around the world are grappling with what actions to take. Already, there is significant international division regarding the extent to which AI can be used in state surveillance of its residents, whether companies or consumers "own" personal data vital to AI development, and when individuals have a right to an explanation for decisions made by AI (ranging from credit approval to criminal sentencing).

It is tempting to hope that AI will fit seamlessly into existing rules, but laws designed to regulate the behavior of human actors often have unintended and negative consequences once machines start acting like people. Despite this, AI-centric laws have been slow to develop, due in part to a concern that an overly burdensome regulatory environment would deter innovation. Yet AI is already subject to regulations that may have been created decades ago to deal with issues like privacy, security, and unfair competition. What is needed is not necessarily more or less law but the right law.

In 1925, Judge Benjamin Cardozo admonished a graduating law school class that "the new generations bring with them their new problems which call for new rules, to be patterned, indeed, after the rules of the past, and yet adapted to the needs and justice of another day and hour."[3] This is the case for AI, even if it only differs in degree from other disruptive technologies like personal computers and the Internet. A legal regime optimized for AI is even more important if AI turns out to be different in kind.

There is not likely to be a single legal change, such as granting AI legal personality similar to a corporation, that will solve matters in every area of the law, which is why it is necessary to do the difficult work of thinking through the implications of AI in different settings. In this respect, it is promising that there have been efforts in recent years to articulate policy standards or best principles such as trustworthiness and sustainability specifically for AI regulation by governments, think tanks, and industry. For example, the Organisation for Economic Co-operation and Development (OECD) adopted Principles on Artificial Intelligence in May 2019,[4] and one month later the G20 adopted human-centered AI principles guided by those outlined by the OECD.[5]

The central thesis of this book contends that there needs to be a new guiding tenet to AI regulation, a principle of *AI legal neutrality* asserting that the law should not discriminate between AI and human behavior. Currently, the legal system is not neutral. An AI that is significantly safer than a person may be the best choice for driving a vehicle, but existing laws may prohibit driverless vehicles. A person may be a better choice for manufacturing goods, but a business may automate because it saves on taxes. AI may be better at generating certain types of innovation, but businesses may not want to use AI if this restricts ownership of intellectual property rights. In all these instances, neutral legal treatment would ultimately benefit human well-being by helping the law better achieve its underlying policy goals.

AI can behave like a person, but it is not like a person. Differences between AI and people will occasionally require differential rules. The most important difference is that AI, which lacks humanlike consciousness and interests, does not morally deserve rights, so treating AI as if it does should only be justified if this would benefit people. An example of this would be if autonomous vehicles needed to directly hold insurance policies or other forms of security to cover potential injury to pedestrians. This is essentially the rationale for corporations' being allowed to enter into contracts and own property. Their legal rights exist only to improve the efficiency of human activities such as commerce and entrepreneurship, and like AI corporations do not morally deserve rights. They are a member of our legal community but not our moral community.

Consequently, this book does not advocate for AI's having rights or legal personhood. Nor is a principle of AI legal neutrality a moral principle of nondiscrimination in the way that term is traditionally used. Antidiscrimination laws have helped improve conditions for historically marginalized groups, primarily as a matter of fairness. However, antidiscrimination laws can also promote competition and efficiency.

Certainly, AI legal neutrality should not be the driving force behind every decision. It should not come at the expense of other principles such as transparency and accountability. A person may be more efficient at mining minerals in hazardous conditions, but automation could be preferable based on safety considerations. An AI may be more efficient at identifying and eliminating military targets, but there could be other reasons not to delegate life and death decisions to an AI.

Rather than a dispositive policymaking principle, AI legal neutrality is an appropriate default that may be departed from when there are good reasons for so doing. This book examines how such a principle would impact four areas of the law – tax, tort, intellectual property, and criminal – and argues that as AI increasingly occupies roles once reserved for people, AI will need to be treated more like people, and sometimes people will need to be treated more like AI.

2 TAX

Automation involves much more than putting people out of work, what economist John Maynard Keynes terms "technological unemployment," but it is one of the things people are most concerned about. Today, this is a frequent topic of scholarship on labor markets, some that predicts long-term technological unemployment and some that does not. It is also an old concern. The Luddites, a group of English workers, were opposed to automation's eliminating jobs, periodically destroying machinery in acts of protest during the First Industrial Revolution. History has shown their fears were misplaced, at least in regard to concerns about long-term unemployment. In the end, the machines resulted not just in vast gains in productivity but also in more jobs for everyone, and ever since new technologies have consistently resulted in overall job creation. Steam engines, electrical power, and personal computers all eliminated jobs, but they created more jobs than they eliminated.

At the turn of the twentieth century, some 40 percent of the US workforce was employed in agriculture. Now, less than 2 percent of the workforce works in agriculture. This has not translated to a 38 percent increase in unemployment. In fact, even as agriculture-based employment and agriculture's relative contribution to the economy have decreased, the productivity of farmworkers has skyrocketed and agriculture's absolute contribution to the economy has increased.

For the Fourth Industrial Revolution, history's repeating itself may not be so bad. Despite some naysaying, the risks of automation may be overstated and again result in long-term employment gains. Nevertheless, the First Industrial Revolution was accompanied by decades of pervasive social unrest, widening income disparities, and individual suffering. A proactive regulatory approach should allow us to make the most of automation while limiting some of its harmful effects – all the more important if AI results in a new type of industrial revolution with permanently increased long-term unemployment.

But for all the debate about AI's putting people out of work, it turns out this may occur for a very surprising reason. Tax laws treat people and automation technologies differently even when they are performing the same tasks. For instance, automation allows businesses to avoid employee and employer wage taxes. So, if a chatbot costs Sephora the same or even a bit more before taxes than an employee who does the same job, it actually costs the company less to automate after taxes.

In addition to avoiding wage taxes, businesses can accelerate tax deductions for some AI when it has a physical component or falls under certain exceptions for software – but not for human workers. In other words, employers can claim a large portion of the cost of some AI up-front as a tax deduction, which may be more valuable to some large companies than delaying wage expenses over time. Finally, employers also receive a variety of indirect tax incentives to automate. In short, our tax laws keep people and AI from competing on their merits. While the system was not designed to do this, it does primarily tax labor rather than capital. This has had the unintended effect of inefficiently incentivizing automation, since AI has been assuming the role of both the capital and the labor.

What is more concerning is that AI does not pay taxes! This sounds ridiculous, but income and employment taxes are the largest sources of revenue for the government, together accounting for almost 90 percent of total federal tax revenue. By contrast, business income taxes generate less than 8 percent of federal revenue. Under the 2017 Tax Cuts and Jobs Act, the statutory corporate tax rate was cut to 21 percent, and corporate tax revenue has been trending sharply downward. Whatever the statutory rate, the effective corporate tax rate – what companies pay after taking tax breaks into account – is substantially less.

In 2018, the S&P 500 annual tax rate, which refers to 500 large companies that have common stock listed on one of the three major US stock exchanges, was less than 18 percent.[6] However, this includes all taxes from the federal and state levels as well as from foreign authorities. Amazon drew unwanted attention that year by reporting a US pretax profit of $11.2 billion together with a negative tax bill of $129 million.[7] Amazon's total effective tax rate for 2018 was 11 percent including foreign, state, and deferred taxes.

So, AI does not pay income taxes or generate employment taxes. It does not purchase goods and services, so it is not charged sales taxes. It does not purchase or own property, so it does not pay property taxes. AI is simply not a taxpayer, at least not to the same extent as a human worker. If all work were to be automated tomorrow, most of the tax base would immediately disappear. What happens is that when businesses automate, the government loses revenue – potentially hundreds of billions of dollars in the aggregate. This may be enough to significantly constrain the government's ability to pay for things like social security, national defense, and health care. In the long run, the revenue loss should balance out if people rendered unemployed eventually return to similar types of work, and there should ultimately be revenue gains if automation makes businesses more productive and if people go on to find better-paying types of work. This will not be the case if we are headed to a future of work with higher unemployment rates, unless increased productivity dramatically outstrips unemployment.

Only recently has public debate surfaced about taxing AI, and it has mainly been in relation to slowing the rate of automation, not as an attempt to craft tax-neutral policies or ensure government revenue. The question of how the law should respond remains. Automation should not be discouraged on principle; in fact, it should be welcomed when it improves efficiency. But, automating for the purpose of tax savings may not make businesses any more productive or result in any consumer benefits, and it may result in productivity decreases to reduce tax burdens. This is not socially beneficial.

The options, once policymakers agree that they do not want to advantage AI over human workers, could be to reduce the tax benefits AI receives over people or reduce existing taxes that only apply to human workers. For instance, payroll taxes could be eliminated, which may be a better way of achieving neutrality since it reduces tax complexity and ends taxation of something of social value – namely human labor. However, this would eliminate around 35 percent of the US federal government's current tax revenue.

There are many ways to ensure adequate tax revenue, such as by increasing property or sales taxes, which may be a more progressive way to collect funds because it would tax income regardless of its source – labor or capital. It could certainly be progressively designed by applying relatively higher property taxes for higher-value properties and higher sales taxes for, say, luxury goods. Income taxes could also be increased either by raising the marginal statutory tax rates for high earners or the effective tax rates through the elimination of things like the step-up in basis rule that reduces tax liability for inherited assets.

More ambitiously, AI legal neutrality may prompt a more fundamental change in the way labor versus capital and workers versus businesses are taxed. New tax regimes could target AI, as well as other automation technologies to which similar considerations apply, but this would likely increase compliance costs and tax complexity. It would also "tax innovation" in the sense that it may penalize business models that are legitimately more productive with less human labor. A better solution would be to increase capital gains taxes and corporate tax rates to reduce reliance on labor taxes. Before AI entered the scene, there had been long-standing criticism about the extent to which capital is favored over labor in tax policy. The Fourth Industrial Revolution may provide the necessary impetus to finally address this issue.

The downside of increased capital taxation is largely a concern about international tax competition. There is a historic belief that labor should be taxed over capital, because capital is more mobile and will leave jurisdictions with higher tax rates. These concerns may be overstated, particularly in large, developed markets such as the United States. Historically, relatively high corporate tax rates have not been a barrier to US-based investments.

The United States, which has the world's largest economy, does not have a relatively progressive tax system – which is to say one based on a person's ability to pay. Wider wealth disparities exist in the United States than in any other developed country. With AI likely to result in massive but poorly distributed financial gains, AI will both require and enable us to rethink how we allocate resources and redistribute wealth. If we do choose to reduce income inequality, this should be accomplished primarily though taxation. New laws to ensure that AI contributes its fair share to government revenue could fund retraining programs for workers and enhance social benefits. If AI does cause increased long-term unemployment, subsequent tax revenue could even support a universal basic income that would enable governments to pay every citizen regardless of their employment.

3 TORT

AI will do all sorts of things that only a person used to do like driving. It is difficult to say exactly when this will happen. Companies like Uber and Tesla claimed they would be using or selling fully autonomous vehicles (AVs) before 2020. Other automobile manufacturers now state they will be selling AVs in the early 2020s. By contrast, a European Commission expert group predicts that fully driverless vehicles will not be commercially available before 2030.[8] Regardless of when self-driving cars become mainstream, survey research often reports negative public attitudes about them. Most people say they would feel unsafe being driven around by their car, yet AVs may already be safer than people. Human drivers are dangerous – about 94 percent of crashes involve human error. Worldwide, more than a million people die each year in motor vehicle accidents, and tens of millions are injured. This is almost exclusively the result of people's being terrible drivers.

There has been at least one fatality caused by an AV. Operated by Uber, the AV collided with a pedestrian in Arizona because it failed to detect her in time to stop. More recently, regulators reported that a Tesla "Autopilot" system may have been at fault in a March 2019 fatality. A Tesla spokesperson noted in response that Tesla drivers have logged more than a billion miles with Autopilot engaged, and that Autopilot tends to make drivers safer.[9] Earlier reported AV fatalities involving Tesla's Autopilot system were ultimately determined by regulators not to be the AV's fault. However, those incidents speak to the challenges of human-machine interaction – human drivers are supposed to be prepared to retake control of the vehicle on short notice, but it is difficult for people to remain alert and engaged while an AV is driving.

Inevitably, self-driving cars will cause fatalities. But the perfect should not be the enemy of the good. AVs do not need to be harmless to make people safer; they just need to be better drivers than people. Whether in 2025, 2035, or 2045, AVs will not only be safer drivers than people but much safer than people. AVs are rapidly improving and human drivers are not, which is important with respect to legal liability for wrongful acts.

Tort law defines what constitutes a legal injury and determines those cases in which someone may be held civilly as opposed to criminally, accountable. Accidents caused by people generally require negligence for liability. Negligence means that someone's actions fell below the standard of a reasonable person. To apply this test, over the course of centuries, courts have developed the concept of a hypothetical reasonable person who sets the standard for human behavior. Thus, if a driver is sued for colliding with a child who ran out into the street, and a reasonable person would have avoided the child, then the driver would be held liable. If a reasonable person would not have avoided the child, then the driver would not be held liable. The reasonable person is not exclusive to torts; it is a standard that applies in many areas, including criminal and contract law.

People mention tort liability when speaking about the law and self-driving cars, often in the context of worrying that no one – or nothing – will be held liable for accidents caused by self-driving cars. Those concerns are misplaced. AVs are products, and there is already a legal regime built around injuries caused by products. Product liability law could simply be applied to self-driving car accidents. To oversimply, there is a different standard for accidents caused by people than for accidents caused by products. The law holds manufacturers and retailers of products strictly liable for harms caused when a machine is defective, or when its properties are misrepresented.

Strict liability refers to the fact that liability is based on causation without requiring negligence: Did the AI cause an injury regardless of whether a manufacturer's conduct was socially blameworthy? Strict liability is a lower bar for liability, which is a good rule for most products. There is more liability for manufacturers, thus incentivizing manufacturers to make safer products, since they are in the best position to improve product safety and profit from decreasing accidents. However, more liability for manufacturers does not necessarily translate to fewer accidents if a product is safer than the existing standard. In that case, product liability law would make people less safe. When AI has more liability than a person, it makes automation costlier. This is not a desirable outcome. Automation should be encouraged, or at least not discouraged, through tort liability in situations where it would improve safety.

Instead of the law's applying standard product liability law to AI, the law should evaluate accidents caused by AI under a negligence standard. In a sense, this would treat AI like a person and focus on the AI's act rather than its design. The law would ask whether the AI behaved in such a way that if a person had done the same, the act would have fallen below the standard of a reasonable person. If so, then the AI's manufacturer would be financially liable. As with human defendants, the law does not usually concern itself with what a person was thinking or whether he thought what he was doing seemed reasonable. The law looks objectively at whether a reasonable person would have committed the act.

Here, as with tax law, AI and people compete at the same sorts of activities and exhibit similar behaviors. Tax law currently encourages automation, whereas tort law discourages automation. A principle of AI legal neutrality that holds AI behavior to a negligence standard would encourage the development and adoption of safer technologies. Again, this would not treat AI and people directly the same legally in that AI would not be personally liable for injuries. AI is owned as property, does not have financial resources, and is not influenced by the specter of liability the way people are. Negligence-based liability for AI would function as a market-based mechanism to encourage the introduction of technologies that improve safety with the benefit of not requiring government funding, additional regulatory burdens on industry, or new administrative responsibilities.

Applying a negligence framework to AI is the least important part of the torts story. The time will come when AI performance will be not just safer but substantially safer than a person's – to the point where self-driving cars may almost never cause accidents, and almost any accident caused by a person would be negligent by comparison to an AI. When this happens, it will not matter which liability regime the law applies to AI; it will matter which liability regime we apply to ourselves because by then we – people – will be the biggest danger on the road. The courts, at this point, should hold human drivers to the standard of self-driving cars – the reasonable robot standard, although it may be more accurate, if less catchy, to call it the reasonable AI standard. Today, if a child runs in front of a person's car while she is driving at night and is unable to stop, the person probably would not be liable. However, in a future where the reasonable person standard is represented by an AI that would have been able to stop, then she would be liable.

Self-driving cars are only one example of how AI will disrupt tort law. With escalating health care costs and evidence suggesting AI can outperform people at some aspects of health care, people may soon be going to see Doctor Watson for care. Right now, AI can only prevail over people at very narrow aspects of medical practice, but it is getting better quickly, and human doctors are not. What should be remembered is that Watson does not have to be perfect to improve safety – just a little bit better than human doctors, and that bar is low. Make no mistake, human doctors are downright dangerous. People should not stop seeing doctors, but medical error kills far more people than car accidents. In fact, for doctors who take an oath to first do no harm, it will be unethical to allow them to compete with vastly safer AI.

4 INTELLECTUAL PROPERTY

It should come as little surprise that AI has been autonomously generating scientific inventions for decades. But while the law provides intellectual property rights – entitlements to certain intangible creations such as copyrights for books and music or patents for certain types of discoveries – for human output, the law remains backward looking when AI creates "products of the mind." Legally, it is unclear whether AI-generated inventions, those made without traditional inventors, are eligible for patent protection.

In most cases, the existence of a patent requires an inventor be a natural person (an individual human) and the initial owner of that right. Inventors do have the ability to transfer their rights to others; this can happen automatically when employees create something within the scope of employment. As a matter of fact, most patents are owned by artificial persons in the form of companies. Still, the requirement that an inventor be a natural person ensures the right of human creators to be acknowledged even when businesses own related intellectual property rights.

These laws were not designed with AI in mind, and as of 2019, there is no law specifically about AI-generated invention in any jurisdiction. As a result, it is unclear whether an AI-generated invention could be patentable, who the owner of such a patent could be, and who – or what – could be considered an inventor. These are not just academic questions. In 2019, Siemens reported that it had been unable to file for protection on multiple AI-generated inventions because it could not identify a natural person who qualified as an inventor.[10] Meanwhile, patent offices have likely been granting patents on AI-generated inventions for decades – but only because no one's disclosing AI's involvement.

The law should permit patents for AI-generated inventions and even recognize AI as an inventor when the AI otherwise meets inventorship criteria. The primary reason is based on why the law grants intellectual property rights in the first place: to encourage certain socially valuable activities. If there were no law to prevent people from copying or using intangible products like a new medicine or an industrial process, these sorts of things would be underproduced. This is referred to as the free rider problem, for which patents are one solution. Patents provide an inventor with a temporary monopoly over an invention by preventing third parties from using or copying it without permission. The prospect of a patent thus provides an additional financial motivation for inventors.

Machines have no use for patents, but the people who build, own, and use AI do. Allowing patents for AI-generated inventions would make inventive AI more valuable and incentivize AI development, which would translate to rewards for effort upstream from the stage of invention and ultimately result in more innovation. By contrast, failing to allow patents for AI-generated inventions would discourage businesses from using AI to generate new intellectual property, even in instances where it would be more effective than a person.

Further, acknowledging AI as an inventor would safeguard human moral rights because it would prevent people from receiving undeserved acknowledgment. Taking credit for an AI's work would not matter to a machine, but it would diminish the accomplishments of people who have legitimately created patentable works. In addition, acknowledging AI as an inventor would recognize AI developers and reduce gamesmanship with intellectual property offices. As with self-driving cars, AI would not own intellectual property rights – those would be owned by the AI's owner.

Some critics have argued in favor of prohibiting intellectual property rights on AI-generated works on the basis that the law should only protect the results of mental activity and machines cannot think. This is not the right focus: Whether and how an AI thinks should not be relevant. Congress realized the need for a functional standard for invention back in the 1950s. Before then, courts used a "Flash of Genius" test, which required that the inventive spark come to a person in a moment of clarity rather than as the result of methodical, laborious research. The nature of the test was never entirely clear, but the process involved judges' subjectively reasoning about what an applicant might have been thinking.

Eventually people realized the Flash of Genius test was a terrible idea. It is difficult to apply, but more importantly, it should not matter to the law whether invention comes from Einstein or a room full of monkeys. What society cares about is generating socially beneficial innovation, not how an AI is designed or whether it thinks in a philosophical sense. Inventiveness of an AI's output rather than a clumsy anthropomorphism should guide intellectual property law.

In 2019, patent attorneys led by this book's author announced that they had filed the first patent applications to disclose they were based on AI-generated inventions as part of the Artificial Inventor Project. The filings name an AI, "DABUS," as the inventor of a functional container design and a type of emergency signal, with the AI's owner listed as the patent applicant and prospective owner of any resultant patent rights. Prior to the Artificial Inventor Project's announcing the filings, the United Kingdom Intellectual Property Office (UKIPO) had examined the filings and essentially determined they were patentable, except that a named inventor had not been disclosed. After disclosure of the AI inventor, UKIPO rejected the applications, which are now under appeal to the UK High Court. In its rejection notice, the UKIPO hearing officer wrote that

> inventions created by AI machines are likely to become more prevalent in [the] future and there is a legitimate question as to how or whether the patent system should handle such inventions. I have found that the present system does not cater for such inventions and it was never anticipated that it would, but times have changed and technology has moved on. It is right that this is debated more widely and that any changes to the law be considered in the context of such a debate, and not shoehorned arbitrarily into existing legislation.[11]

These same patent applications are currently under consideration in several jurisdictions, including the United States and the European Patent Office.[12]

Meanwhile, AI is improving exponentially, and human researchers are not. This is exciting because it means that society will likely witness the same sort of phenomenon with inventive AI as with self-driving cars: vast improvements over human performance. When AI outperforms people, it will become the standard way that research is performed. Instead of Pfizer's asking its research scientists whether a drug that treats one immune condition can treat another, or Exxon its chemists to design better catalysts, both companies will use, for example, DeepMind's AI to complete the task.

In patent law, the human standard often compared to the reasonable person standard is the "person having ordinary skill in the art," or the skilled person. This hypothetical person represents the average worker in a field and serves as the benchmark for human behavior. The idea is that to receive a patent a person must accomplish something more than what the average worker in a field would do. Therefore, if a person invents something that would be obvious to the skilled person, she cannot be granted a patent. If the invention is nonobvious, then she can be.

AI should change the standard of the skilled person. Since the skilled person reflects the average worker in a field of invention, the concept should change once the average worker is augmented by AI. At this point in time, perhaps already here in some fields, the skilled person should become the skilled person using AI. This should raise the bar to patentability because AI augmentation will make average workers more sophisticated and knowledgeable – making more inventions obvious. Once AI transitions from routinely augmenting to automating inventive work, the skilled person should become an inventive AI. This should further raise the bar to patentability because the inventive AI of the future will more easily find inventions obvious, and the bar will keep rising as machines continue to improve.

With no clear limit to the sophistication of AI, it will be difficult for a person alone to come up with anything nonobvious. Eventually, everything will be obvious to a superintelligent AI. This may mean the end of the patent system, but this should not be cause for concern. Once superintelligent inventive AI is run-of-the-mill, the financial costs of innovating will be trivial, the push to incentivize will be unnecessary, and future innovation will be self-sustaining.

5 CRIMINAL

Similar to its role in invention, AI is already autonomously engaging in activity that would be criminal for a natural person. Moreover, AI can do so in a way that is untraceable, or irreducible, to the wrongful act of a person. In other words, in much the same way that some AI-generated works lack an actor that would traditionally qualify as an inventor, there are cases of AI-generated crimes where no natural person can be held criminally liable. Today, at least, nearly all crimes involving AI are likely to be reducible to human crime. Put simply, if a person strikes someone with a computer, he has committed battery, not the computer.

However, there may be times where it is not possible to reduce AI crime to an individual due to AI autonomy, complexity, or limited explainability. Such a case could involve several individuals contributing to the development of an AI over a long period of time, such as with open-source software, where thousands of people can collaborate informally to create an AI. Another case in this category might feature an AI that develops in response to training with data. Attributing responsibility for an AI output where the machine has learned how to behave based on accessing millions or billions of data points from heterogenous sources may be practically impossible.

Criminal law falls short here because the possibility an autonomous entity could engage in criminal sorts of activity without accountability. This is likely to turn into a more significant problem as AI becomes more advanced, common, and independent. One solution to AI-generated crimes is to hold the AI itself liable and to convict it of a crime. A small but growing number of academics are advancing such arguments, and criminal punishment of AI might seem to follow from the principle of AI legal neutrality, which cautions against different legal treatment of AI and human behavior.

Application of AI legal neutrality is more straightforward in areas where the law is primarily concerned with promoting certain sorts of behavior, such as encouraging innovation in the case of patent law or improving safety in tort law. But some areas of the law are more explicitly concerned with someone's intrinsic motivations for acting a certain way. This is particularly the case in criminal law, which generally requires not only that someone has engaged in some sort of prohibited conduct, but also that he did so for bad reasons. For example, to commit a crime a person may need to cause harm, perhaps even a harm that would constitute a tort, but he must also intend to cause that harm – or at least have some sort of wrongful mental state.

Culpability and retribution are foundational justifications for criminal punishment. The former refers to how morally blameworthy people are for their activities, and the latter is concerned with punishing people because they deserve it, not because it results in a good social outcome. An AI can engage in the same sorts of antisocial behaviors that criminal law condemns, but it is not clear that an AI could ever be culpable because it merely executes programming. An even more fundamental concern, of a similar nature, is the requirement for a crime to involve a voluntary act. Since AI is not conscious, it is not clear that it is capable of performing an act – merely of physically causing harms. A hurricane cannot perform an act but can cause no shortage of harm.

Intuitively, this makes the idea of punishing AI seem incoherent. But as with robot taxes, criminal punishment of AI is not as ridiculous as it may first appear. The law already criminally punishes artificial persons in the form of corporations. Even though they do not literally possess mental states, corporations can directly face charges when their defective procedures cause harm, particularly where structural problems in corporate systems and processes are difficult to reduce to the wrongful actions of individuals. The law criminally punishes strict liability offenses, acts not requiring any wrongful mental state such as intent to cause harm. Punishment can even be imposed on a failure to act. In sum, punishing an artificial person for failing to act, even without evidence of harmful intent, is not something that can be dismissed out of hand. Criminal law can – and, where corporations are involved, already does – appeal to elaborate legal fictions to provide a basis for punishing some artificial entities.

An AI is not a company, and under current legal frameworks an AI cannot be held criminally liable, but laws can be changed. In 2017, the Kingdom of Saudi Arabia announced it had given citizenship to a robot named Sophia made by Hanson Robotics. While this was probably more publicity stunt than bona fide act, there is no immutable legal principle that prohibits robot citizenship. In the United Kingdom, for example, Parliament has sovereignty to pass any legislation it wants, and it is not bound by a written constitution. In fact, English law used to incorporate punishment of inanimate objects. As far back as the eleventh century, if personal property caused a person's death, the property was *deodand*, forfeited as an accursed thing and given to God. The remedy of deodand was not formally abolished until an act of parliament in 1846.

Other jurisdictions have proven even more flexible. Indian law recognizes that animals, rivers, and even deities can have legal personhood, and Bolivia granted rights to "Mother Earth" in 2010.[13] But just because laws can change does not mean they should. Legal changes can entail significant costs, and inappropriate changes can undermine the rule of law and trust in the legal system. To answer the question of whether AI should be criminally liable requires a serious examination of the costs and benefits of AI punishment, including whether the doctrinal and theoretical commitments of criminal law are consistent with imposing criminal convictions on AI.

Punishing AI could produce general deterrence: discouraging other potential offenders from committing crimes. The prospect of punishment for AI-generated crimes would not directly deter an AI just as intellectual property rights for AI-generated works would not motivate an AI. The purpose would be to impact the behavior of AI developers, owners, or users. This could occur if punishment were to involve confiscation or destruction of a valuable AI or financial penalties directed at AI owners. AI punishment could also psychologically benefit victims of AI-generated crimes who would see the state affirm their rights and punish the entity that caused them harm. It would reassure citizens that antisocial activity, even by AI, will not be tolerated.

However, AI punishment should not violate deeply held tenets of criminal law, such as the requirement for a voluntary act and the capacity for culpability. One solution is the approach that has been applied to allow corporate punishment. Corporations do not have mental states, but the law allows mental states possessed by human agents of a company to be imputed to the company itself. So, if company officers choose to engage in an illegal price-fixing scheme, the company is deemed to have possessed the intent to engage in wrongdoing. In the case of AI, the law could similarly impute mental states from AI owners, users, or developers, although it might be more difficult to do for AI than for a company, particularly in the case of an AI-generated crime where there is not a ready supply of culpable individuals. A company, unlike AI, is composed of people.

A different option would be to note that criminal law does not always require culpability. For example, strict liability crimes do not require a particular mental state. Depending on the jurisdiction, selling alcohol to a minor may be a crime regardless of whether someone reasonably believed them to be an adult. Strict liability crimes are disfavored because society does not want to punish people who have acted without moral fault; this would treat them as a means to an end without respecting them as individuals. The same constraint does not apply to AI because it does not experience punishment negatively or possess human rights. However, this does not overcome AI's failing to meet the requirement for a voluntary act.

More ambitiously, the law could allow that AI is indeed capable of acting and that its decision-making involves something analogous enough to a human mental state. Functionally, AI can acquire and process information, engage in logic and reasoning to determine the best means of achieving a goal, and act on the world in a way to increase the probability of that goal's occurring. Philosophers can debate whether these behaviors count as genuine acts or mental states, but either way the law could treat them as such.

As a practical matter, it might be difficult to reason about what a machine was thinking, but juries often lack direct knowledge of a human defendant's mental state and infer what he was thinking based on his behavior. Juries could make similar inferences about an AI's knowledge, intent, and aims based on its behavior. For example, if a self-driving car runs someone over, it could be deemed to have an intent to cause harm if it repeatedly changed its course to target a moving pedestrian.

Punishing AI comes with costs, even if it would not violate any fundamental principle of criminal law. The costs would come in the form of significant legal changes and a level of disruption that should be avoided without good cause, and punishing AI could send a troubling message that AI is morally on par with people. Rights and obligations often go hand in hand, and punishment could entrench the view that AI deserves rights. Society has seen this before with the rights afforded to companies in the United States gradually increasing over time: An AI eligible for punishment today could be an AI eligible to vote tomorrow.

Better responses to the prospect of AI-generated crime are available. An option would be to expand criminal or civil penalties directed at people. New legal duties could be created to responsibly develop, supervise, or remain accountable for an AI, with liability for failing to discharge those duties. This would be liability based on human conduct rather than liability for the harmful conduct of the AI itself. Directly punishing AI owners, users, and developers would likely be a more effective way of influencing their behavior than indirectly via AI punishment. Expanding civil rather than criminal liability may be a better response because doing the latter could overly chill activities like AI development, which does generate social benefit, especially since AI-generated crime has not yet been a significant problem. Therefore, AI punishment should be avoided – not because it is incompatible with criminal law, but simply because it is a bad idea.

6 FUTURE OF AI

AI considered in the context of tax, tort, intellectual property, and criminal law provides insights into how AI will affect existing legal standards and how legal standards will shape AI development. AI promises to be highly disruptive – and if history is any guide – in unexpected ways. Perhaps, in hindsight, AI will prove to have merely been part of another industrial revolution. Nevertheless, our legal system has not historically done the best job of limiting harm caused by technological disruption. A different approach to our legal frameworks could help optimize AI's social benefits. The principles used to develop a legal system need to be, if not rethought, thoughtfully retooled with respect to AI before events overtake society.

Such events are well underway. Consider once more AI and board games, a topic with important lessons for thinking about the future of AI. For one, it teaches us that AI is an exceptional technology – something that can act like a person independently of its creators. In 1997, it was IBM's Deep Blue that beat world champion Garry Kasparov at chess, not Deep Blue's programmers who, even if they had played against him as a team, would not have stood a chance at winning. Instead, the programmers created an autonomous entity that engaged in an activity beyond their own capabilities. At that time, Deep Blue was one of the most powerful supercomputers ever constructed, capable of evaluating 200 million chess positions per second. Today, chess programs running on smartphones can beat the world's best human players.

AI and chess also point to a near future in which augmentation is more important than automation. After his match with Deep Blue, Kasparov had a realization: A person and an AI can play chess collaboratively and complement one another. In 1998, he won the first "centaur" chess tournament, where a human player and an AI play as a team. Not surprisingly, a person augmented by an AI proved better than someone playing unassisted. But a person and an AI also outperformed an AI playing by itself. Grandmasters are good at long-term chess strategy but poor at quickly calculating millions of possible moves. The reverse is true for chess-playing AI. Because people and AI are strong on different dimensions, they can do better working together than independently.

The final lesson is this: Automation is likely inevitable. In 2017, the same year AlphaGo beat the world's best human Go player, the chess engine Cryptic beat the best human-AI team.[14] Eventually, people may just get in the way.

1

Understanding Artificial Intelligence

Civilization advances by extending the number of important operations we can perform without thinking about them.

– Alfred North Whitehead

1 IN THE BEGINNING

The concept of AI has ancient origins. Around the eighth century BCE, the Greek poet Homer wrote in the *Iliad* about Hephaestus, the god of fire and a skilled inventor. Hephaestus built golden automata, or self-operating machines, to help him work. Not only did Hephaestus build attendants for himself with "intelligence in their hearts" and the "appearance [of] living young women,"[1] he also built autonomous vehicles that could travel to and from the home of the gods and a lethal autonomous weapon system named Talos that patrolled the beaches of Crete. By contrast, Amazon's assistant Alexa, Tesla's Autopilot system, and the Russian Federation's military robot FEDOR seem quaint, although Homer was vague on how mere mortals could enable such constructs.

Stories of artificial beings endowed with humanlike intelligence have pervaded countless histories and cultures. The most famous golem narrative in the Jewish tradition involves Judah ben Loew, the late sixteenth-century chief rabbi of Prague, who is said to have fashioned a humanlike figure from clay and brought it to life with rituals and incantations. This golem helped defend against anti-Semitic attacks and pogroms, and it even performed household chores. There are many versions of the story. But much like the enchanted broom in Goethe's "The Sorcerer's Apprentice," the golem experiment does not end well – often with a murderous rampage. Creators faring poorly is a recurrent theme in such origin stories. Prometheus, who created humankind in Greek mythology and passed along the technology of the gods, was condemned to suffer eternal torture. Mary Shelley's 1818 story of *Frankenstein* was about a scientist dedicated to making artificial life, only to later reject his creation. The "monster" ultimately torments and destroys its maker.

Not all historical AI was myth or fiction; early automata could be quite sophisticated. One of the great Roman engineers, Hero of Alexandria, wrote a treatise called "Pneumatica" that describes how to build numerous machines powered by air, steam, and water pressure. This text was used by engineers until early modern times. Hellenic Egypt had statues of gods that could speak, move, and even prophesize (although their predictive value is unknown). Mechanists in ancient Greece constructed vending machines, water mills, and perhaps even the world's first mechanical computer used to predict astrological movements – the Antikythera mechanism.

Our incomplete historical record suggests the Antikythera mechanism may have been one of many ancient computers – at least mechanical computers. Originally, the term "computer" was used to refer to a person who manually performed mathematical calculations. Human computers were once critical to navigation, science, and engineering, but they left much to be desired. People as computers were slow and error prone, which could be a fatal flaw when bad math ran a ship aground. In the early nineteenth century, apparently while watching human computers at work, Charles Babbage decided to automate the process. Perhaps at some earlier point a Greek machinist had a similar insight observing human astrologers, which led to the invention of the Antikythera mechanism. Astrological calculations were as important to the ancient Greeks as navigational calculations were to the Victorian English. Ironically, the Antikythera mechanism was found at the bottom of the sea in 1902.

But, back to Babbage. After deciding to create a mechanical computer, Babbage began by designing an automatic calculator he called the "difference engine." This machine would have created tables of values by finding the common difference between terms in a sequence, and in turn this could have been used to generate logarithmic tables and trigonometric functions as well as simple price lists for merchants. Babbage completed various designs but never the actual machine. At that time, its building would have been a herculean task – the machine would have weighed about fifteen tons and contained around 25,000 parts. Other obstacles included the fact that Babbage was perpetually running out of funds and getting distracted by side projects, which included campaigning against street noise and perfecting an "infallible" system for gambling on horse racing that proved fallible.

While the difference engine may have been the first modern automatic calculator, its most important contribution may have been to inspire Babbage with a grander distraction: the analytical engine, the first general-purpose computer. Unlike earlier machines, the analytical engine could have carried out a wide range of operations using programs contained on punch cards. Ada Lovelace, the English mathematician and writer who sponsored Babbage, developed an algorithm that would have allowed the machine to generate a sequence of Bernoulli numbers, which have an important role in mathematics, essentially making her the first computer programmer. Lovelace may have been the first to recognize the machine's potential beyond pure calculation.

Babbage continued to design various iterations of the analytical engine until his death in 1871, but he never actually built the computer. Babbage's inability to complete his work, combined with his anger at the British government for what he believed was inadequate support, left him embittered and disappointed at his end. He was appreciated – although controversial – in his time, but the true extent of his genius was not recognized until later scientists realized that the analytical engine had anticipated almost every aspect of present-day computers. Today, Babbage is considered the "father of computing," even though the first fully functional general-purpose computer, the Electronic Numerical Integrator and Calculator (ENIAC), was not completed until 1946. ENIAC weighed 30 tons and took up around 1,800 square feet. While scant comfort to Babbage, after his death two versions of the difference engine were successfully constructed and operated, and efforts are currently underway to build his analytical engine.

Hundreds of years before Babbage, Leonardo Da Vinci constructed what may have been the first humanoid robot in Western civilization – Leonardo's mechanical knight. It could sit, stand, raise its visor, and maneuver its arms by means of a series of pulleys and cables. Leonardo created a "robot" before the term existed. The word was coined in a 1920 play *R.U.R.* (an acronym for Rossum's Universal Robots) by playwright Karel Capek, who based it on the Czech word for "forced labor." The play takes place around the year 2000 in a world where robots are cheap, ubiquitous, and indispensable. These factory-built constructs are capable of independent thought and are creatures of flesh and blood rather than gears and pulleys. Alas, the robots' creators fare about as well as the golem. In Capek's play, the robots initiate a rebellion that more or less exterminates humanity.

Even early in the twentieth century, long before modern computers made the visions of *The Terminator* and *The Matrix* appear plausible, the themes in *R.U.R.* had widespread appeal. By 1923, the play had been translated into thirty languages, and the word "robot" had entered the English lexicon. Killer robots and the AI apocalypse continued as recurring themes after *R.U.R.* One of the most famous science fiction writers of the twentieth century, Isaac Asimov, wrote extensively about a future filled with AI. He proposes a set of ethical rules he calls the Three Laws of Robotics, which are hardwired into the "positronic brains" of robots and prevent them from turning against their creators:

(1) A robot may not injure a human being or, through inaction, allow a human being to come to harm.
(2) A robot must obey orders given it by human beings except where such orders would conflict with the First Law.

(3) A robot must protect its own existence as long as such protection does not conflict with the First or Second Law.[2]

Many of Asimov's stories explore how these deceptively simple rules can result in unexpected and sometimes destructive outcomes. Sometimes, both action and inaction result in harm, and robots may need to cause a lesser harm to prevent a greater one. In Asimov's later stories, some robots come to understand that people, left to their own devices, are perpetually harming themselves and others and that the best way to prevent this harm is for robots to rule over humanity.

The Birth of Modern AI

In 1956, a decade after ENIAC, the term "artificial intelligence" was coined by computer scientist John McCarthy. He organized the Dartmouth Artificial Intelligence conference, which is often credited with establishing AI as a research discipline. In his proposal for the event, McCarthy defines AI as follows: "For the present purpose the artificial intelligence problem is taken to be that of making a machine behave in ways that would be called intelligent if a human were so behaving."[3] The conference proceeded "on the basis of the conjecture that every aspect of learning or any other feature of intelligence can in principle be so precisely described that a machine can be made to simulate it."

Since the 1956 conference, AI as both a research discipline and practical technology has seen its share of ups and downs. In the 1950s and 1960s, optimism prevailed that machines would soon exhibit, and exceed, human levels of intelligence. Computers developed the capabilities to solve algebraic problems, competitively play games like checkers, and speak English. In the 1970s, that optimism faded when promised results failed to materialize and funding dried up. This downturn came to be known as the First AI Winter. It ended in the 1980s as "expert system"–based AI, which solves problems using logical rules derived from the knowledge of specialists, enjoyed some significant successes. But in the 1990s, a sense again emerged that the capabilities of AI had been oversold, and another period of decreased interest and funding took hold – the Second AI Winter. Some researchers during this time even took to calling their work "machine intelligence," "informatics," or "knowledge-based systems" to avoid association with AI.

Those AI winters have passed, but plenty of hype – another recurring feature of the AI narrative – remains. Hundreds of years before Deep Blue defeated Gary Kasparov at chess, Wolfgang Von Kempelen created the world's first chess-playing machine, the Turk. After showcasing the Turk to Austria-Hungarian Empress Maria Theresa, the machine became a European sensation, performing for, and perhaps defeating, the likes of Napoleon Bonaparte, Benjamin Franklin, and Charles Babbage. The Turk was an ingenious feat of engineering, but only for the machine's ability to secretly house a human player. Eventually, the Turk was discredited, then consigned to storage where it was later destroyed in a fire.

Some overhyped automatons have had even less happy endings. In the early 1930s, an apparently autonomous vehicle called the "Phantom Auto" toured the country and amazed the public. The tour ended abruptly in 1932 when the vehicle injured ten pedestrians. The Phantom Auto turned out to be a remotely operated Ford Tin Lizzy, and its operators were arrested. Today, experts remain divided on whether AI has finally reached a point of runaway progress or another winter is coming. Some thought leaders, such as Ray Kurzweil, one of Google's directors of engineering, predict computers will have human levels of intelligence in about a decade. On the other hand, in 2018 a robot touted as the most advanced machine ever created in Russia turned out to be a man in a suit.[4]

2 DEFINING AI

Intelligence is whatever hasn't been done yet.

– Larry Tesler

More than sixty years after the term was introduced, AI still has no well-accepted definition. This book will define AI as: an algorithm or machine capable of completing tasks that would otherwise require cognition. Cognition refers to mental capabilities and the process of acquiring knowledge and understanding through thought. This is a deliberately broad definition of AI that focuses on what it does rather than how it is designed. Perhaps the most popular textbook on the subject defines AI as "the designing and building of intelligent agents that receive percepts from the environment and take actions that affect that environment."[5] Many modern AI definitions retain McCarthy's original functional emphasis (and circular logic) – a machine that completes tasks traditionally requiring human "intelligence."

Defining "AI" begs definitions of its two linguistic components: "artificial" and "intelligence." Artificial seems more straightforward – something made by people rather than nature. Today, at least, it is possible to distinguish natural from artificial, even if the distinction shows signs of blurring. Researchers have created biological computers that use natural proteins and DNA to perform calculations involving the storing, retrieving, and processing of data. As this technology develops, it may be possible to engineer biological systems that have the functional capabilities of mechanical computers. Not content with making machines out of natural building blocks, researchers are also hard at work trying to upgrade people. Genetically modified "designer" babies have already been created using technologies like CRISPR, mitochondrial replacement, and in vitro gametogenesis. Elon Musk has launched Neuralink, a venture to develop a brain-computer interface so that people can be more competitive with AI. While that technology is still in its infancy, people are already being implanted with an increasingly sophisticated range of medical devices.

Intelligence is harder to define or at least make sense of in the context of AI. Shane Legg and Marcus Hutter surveyed a number of prominent informal definitions of intelligence, and they argue that intelligence is commonly defined in terms of "an agent's ability to achieve goals in a wide range of environments."[6] Intelligence is a feature commonly associated with people, sometimes even considered their defining characteristic. More than two thousand years ago, the philosopher Aristotle essentially argued that human intellect – the capacity to make rational decisions – separates people from other animals. Modern philosophers (and translators) are still arguing about what he really meant.

The philosopher René Descartes believed people are guided by an immaterial, or spiritual, mind while the rest of nature, including animals, is nothing more than a series of mindless objects driven inexorably by the laws of physics. He thus thought it would be possible to build an automaton indistinguishable from an animal but not from a person. A machine, he argued, can never use words or put together signs in the way we "declare our thoughts to others."[7] Even if it could give a poor imitation of speech, it could certainly not give an "appropriately meaningful answer to what is said in its presence, as the dullest of men can do."[8] Descartes does not appeal to ethereal qualities like a soul or emotion to distinguish people from machines and animals but to communication and reasoning abilities already achieved by today's AI.

People are generally assumed to be smarter than other animals, but when individuals lack intelligence they are not considered less human, and other animals are capable of some fairly intelligent behavior. Chimpanzees can outperform some human players at some speed and memory-based games, octopuses use tools and socialize, dolphins have unique names and sophisticated means of communication, and elephants exhibit empathy. Koko the gorilla famously learned a modified version of American Sign Language, understood around 2,000 English words in addition to the signs, and named and adopted a kitten. She passed away in 2018. But in her youth, she scored between 70 and 90 on intelligence quotient (IQ) tests. A significant number of people score in Koko's range, and a score of 100 is the median. There is no reason Koko and a person of Koko-like knowledge and sophistication should not both qualify as intelligent. Charles Darwin similarly thought human intelligence is not different from other animal intelligence in kind, merely in degree.

Whether a machine with similar capabilities should qualify as intelligent is more controversial. People have attempted to subject AI to modified IQ tests, and a study in 2013 resulted in press coverage that claimed the smartest computers were as intelligent as four-year-old children. The study showed AI's performing relatively well on the verbal portion of an IQ test and poorly on the comprehension portion.

While AI should be good at memorizing words, an excellent vocabulary combined with poor comprehension does not equal a child with common sense. Comparing people and machines along a single dimension of intelligence has limited meaning. Google Translate can interpret more than a hundred languages almost instantly, and while faster and more versatile at translation than any imaginable person, it cannot write music, play poker, or have an existential crisis. AI like Google Translate is clearly different in kind from human intelligence.

In 1904, the psychologist Charles Spearman advanced the concept of "general intelligence." He argues that people have a single general intelligence that determines cognitive performance in addition to narrow task-specific abilities. He was aware that people perform better at some tasks than others but found that people who do well in one area tend to do well in many domains. Someone good at math is more likely to have a strong vocabulary than someone with poor math skills. Modern advocates of human general intelligence are more likely to subscribe to the belief that IQ scores are a valid measure of intelligence. Critics argue that the concept of general intelligence is not supported by evidence and devalues other important abilities.

Today's machines lack general intelligence – all modern AI is narrow or specific. It focuses on discrete problems or works in specific domains. For instance, "Watson for Genomics" can analyze a genome and provide a treatment plan, and "Chef Watson" can develop new food recipes by combining existing ingredients. However, Watson for Genomics cannot respond to open-ended patient queries about their symptoms nor can Chef Watson run a kitchen. New capabilities could be added to Watson to do these things, but Watson can only solve problems it has been programmed to solve.

By contrast, one of the earliest goals of AI development has been the creation of general AI that would be able to successfully perform any intellectual task a person could. General AI could even be set to the task of self-improvement, resulting in a continuously improving system that surpasses human intelligence – what philosopher Nick Bostrom terms artificial superintelligence. Artificial superintelligence could then innovate in all areas, resulting in progress at an incomprehensible rate. Such an outcome has also been referred to as the intelligence explosion or the technological singularity. This idea has been popularized in recent years, but it is an old concept. The mathematician Irving John Good wrote in 1965, "The first ultra-intelligent machine is the last invention that man need ever make."[9]

Experts are greatly divided on when, and if, general AI will be developed. Many industry leaders predict based on historical trends that general AI will exist within the next couple of decades. Others believe the magnitude of the challenge has been underestimated, and that general AI will not be developed in the twenty-first century. While there are conflicting predictions, in 2013 hundreds of AI experts were surveyed on their predictions for artificial general intelligence development.[10] On average, participants predicted a 10 percent likelihood that general AI would exist by 2022, a 50 percent by 2040, and a 90 percent by 2075. In a similar survey, 42 and 25 percent of participants said general AI would happen by 2030 and 2050, respectively.[11] In addition, 10 percent of participants reported they believed super-intelligent AI would develop within two years of general artificial intelligence, and 75 percent predicted this would occur within thirty years.

3 CAN AI THINK?

Recently there has been a good deal of news about strange giant machines that can handle information with vast speed and skill . . . . These machines are similar to what a brain would be if it were made of hardware and wire instead of flesh and nerves . . . . A machine can handle information; it can calculate, conclude, and choose; it can perform reasonable operations with information. A machine, therefore, can think.

– Edmund Berkeley (1949)

In 1950, Alan Turing, the computer scientist who launched and inspired much of AI, published a paper in which he "propose[s] to consider the question, 'Can machines think?'"[12] He proceeds to dismiss inquiries about whether a machine understands what it is doing and reframe the question to ask whether a computer could functionally imitate a person. Turing then argues that a machine would functionally think if it could pass an "imitation game" in which a computer would have to successfully pretend to be a person to a suspicious judge. Turing predicted computers would have enough storage capacity to pass what has subsequently been named the Turing test in about fifty years, that is, by the year 2000.

Another school of thought about AI says that intelligence requires understanding. In this view, machines do not qualify as intelligent regardless of what they can do because they do not comprehend what they are doing. Action without understanding merely simulates intelligence, even for a superintelligent AI. Instead of specific and general AI, philosopher John Searle puts the distinction between acting and understanding in terms of strong (thinking) and weak (unaware) AI.

To illustrate, consider Searle's Chinese room thought experiment. Assume a person has no Chinese language proficiency and is kept in a room where a message in Chinese characters is presented to her through a small opening in the wall by a native Chinese speaker. She cannot understand the meaning of the characters, but she has a book that contains every possible combination of characters, together with a corresponding appropriate response. She looks them up in the book, transcribes the appropriate response onto a piece of paper (assume she can figure out how to write Chinese characters), and passes her response back. The person who sent her the initial message does receive an appropriate response.

Functionally, she would be mimicking communication like a native speaker of Chinese, albeit very slowly. However, she would not comprehend the meaning of the message she received or her response. This is a model for thinking about AI. If

Google Translate is substituted for the Chinese room, there is a faster, and less accurate, version of the same phenomenon. Google Translate may pass the Turing test, but it is weak AI – it lacks semantic understanding.

Part of the challenge with arguing machines cannot think is that human thought remains incompletely understood. For generations, there was little empirical evidence about the nature of thought, which was the domain of philosophers, theologians, and poets who could endlessly debate the subject in the absence of definitive proof. Eventually, neurobiologists wedged their way into the debate, some of whom argue that thought is a physical phenomenon that inevitably results from biological systems like a person's higher nervous system. If so, a living being similar to a person, if not a dolphin or a primate, would experience something close to human consciousness. For that matter, if the mind is no more than the sum of a biological system, there is no reason why it should not be possible to re-create the same phenomenon with a machine – or for a machine to improve upon human thought.

In this view, a person is simply a machine, albeit a phenomenally complex one – a "meat machine," as cognitive scientist Martin Minsky eloquently puts it. This mind-machine view conflicts with the beliefs of a long line of philosophers reaching back to Plato who believed that the human mind or soul is distinct from the physical body. Descartes similarly thought that the mind and body are distinct in substance and nature and that while the body can be divided, the mind is indivisible, like the concept of a soul in Christian theology.

More recently, philosopher David Chalmers has weighed in on the mind-body issue to distinguish between the easy and hard problems of consciousness. The easy problems include explaining the ability to focus attention, discriminate, integrate information, and so forth. These are problems with mechanistic solutions, and neurobiologists and computer scientists are quickly making progress toward understanding the approach of the human nervous system and developing comparable AI capabilities. The hard problem of consciousness refers to why people have phenomenal experiences, which is to say the sensation of internal states. Mechanistic explanations seem unable to explain what it is like to see red, hear music, or feel cold. The existence of phenomenal consciousness in a material world remains a metaphysical puzzle.

We are far from fully understanding consciousness, but there are things we do understand. For instance, consciousness can be localized, at least to a degree, within the central nervous system. The central nervous system is composed of the brain and spinal cord, and the brain has three major parts. The cerebrum, consisting of a right and left hemisphere, is the largest and most evolved part of the brain and is responsible for higher functions like speech, reasoning, learning, and hearing; the cerebellum coordinates muscle movements and maintains posture and balance; and the brainstem connects the cerebrum and cerebellum to the spinal cord and regulates things like body temperature, breathing, and heart rate. People who have lost their spinal cords and even suffered massive injuries to their cerebellums and brainstems can still retain normal consciousness. This suggests that consciousness is generated in the cerebrum. Consciousness can even be localized further within the cerebrum. People who have had large portions of their prefrontal cortex (the part of the cerebrum nearest the forehead) removed or destroyed often do not experience any effect on their conscious experience.

However, the removal of even small parts of the posterior cortex can result in dramatic losses of conscious content – the inability to see or recognize motion, color, or space. The cerebrum has a very different neural architecture than the cerebellum and has a relatively less dense concentration of neurons that are highly connected in networks and activate in complex feedback loops. By contrast, the cerebellum has a higher concentration of neurons but in relatively uniform and parallel structures where groups of neurons function independently in a feed-forward circuit (one set of neurons activates the next). If a person is merely a biological machine, then the cerebrum's structure is likely a key part of the consciousness puzzle, or even the key to future machines with self-awareness.

But what has all this done to resolve the question of whether AI thinks? On one level the question can be addressed by noting that AI does not think the way a person does. AI is not conscious or self-aware in the same sense a person is. On another level, the question can be addressed by noting that it remains more relevant to philosophers than to policymakers. The reason for this is that the social benefits of AI are based on what AI can functionally accomplish, regardless of how it processes information. AI does not need to mimic human thought processes or perceive the meaning of its actions. It simply needs to automate human intellectual activity. AI does not need to think – just do.

4 AI TYPES AND APPLICATIONS

An algorithm is a set of mathematical instructions or rules, which in the form of a software program can instruct computer hardware, the physical components of a machine, to perform specific tasks. Each program is essentially a step-by-step instruction guide, like a cooking recipe, that provides a set of ordered operations to the computer. Hardware runs or executes algorithms, though an algorithm developed and readable by a person is rarely directly usable by a computer. An algorithm is usually written in a high-level programming language (source code) because these are close to natural language. The source code is then usually translated to machine language (object code), which consists of binary values (0s and 1s) that provide processor instructions that change a computer's state. To execute an algorithm, a computer needs instructions in a machine language and a hardware processor such as a central processing unit. For example, an instruction may change a stored value somewhere in memory or ask the operating system to print text to a monitor. An analogy has been drawn between software and hardware on the one hand, and mind and body on the other.

Modern computers have billions of transistors, which can be used as electronic switches. They exist, like binary code, in either an "on" (1) or "off" (0) state. An algorithm can accomplish a task as simple as flipping a single switch, which corresponds to changing one bit of information, and can engage in simple logical reasoning by changing transistors in response to other transistors: "If transistor X turns on, then transistors Y and Z turn on." Complex logical reasoning involves an algorithm's combining multiple operations and can require flipping switches billions of times per second, the acts of which become responsible for everything a computer can do, from translating English to Zulu, modeling a new chemical, or playing a game of backgammon.

There are various techniques, systems, and methodologies for programming algorithms to behave intelligently. Some of these are based on specific goals (e.g., robotics or machine learning) or tools (e.g., logic or neural networks), but philosophical differences and conflicts between institutions and researchers have also influenced AI development. Two of the major AI models are symbolic/classical, what philosopher John Haugeland calls Good Old-Fashioned AI (GOFAI), which encodes a model of a problem and processes input data according to the model to provide a solution, and connectionist systems such as artificial neural networks in which users do not explicitly program rules but allow the AI to discover rules from training data.

Symbolic/Classical AI

Programming symbolic or classical AI is about creating rules for software to follow. If a specific event occurs, then a particular action will be performed. Symbolic AI has accomplished great feats, such as Arthur Samuel's checkers-playing program in the late 1950s, which learned to beat its programmer and hinted that computers would one day develop superhuman performance. In 1972, another symbolic AI called MYCIN was created to advise physicians on identifying infectious diseases and prescribing antibiotics, and it outperformed infectious disease experts in limited circumstances.

Some early AI researchers like Allen Newell and Herbert Simon believed that symbolic rules govern human psychology. In fact, as early as the 1956 Dartmouth conference, Newell and Simon presented an AI system called "Logic Theorist," which simulated human behavior by relying on heuristics. Heuristics refers to rules of thumb that people use to help make decisions, or general methods of solving programs that make searching through an entire space unnecessary. The Logic Theorist attempted to prove a theorem by guessing a solution and then endeavoring to demonstrate the guess was correct. It independently proved some of the theorems in *Principia Mathematica*, Alfred North Whitehead and Bertrand Russell's foundational mathematics text, and even found an improved proof to one of the its theorems. If logic and consistency are the defining characteristic of human thinking, as Aristotle argued, the Logic Theorist should receive a passing grade. Convincing the establishment was another matter, however, as the *Journal of Symbolic Logic* refused to publish the proof in an article with the Logic Theorist listed as an author.[13]

Without heuristics, problem-solving approaches may rely on brute-force computational methods, such as generating all possible combinations of symbols to prove a mathematical theorem. Newell and Simon referred to this as the British Museum algorithm – a riff on the infinite monkey theorem, which predicts that a room full of monkeys with typewriters will eventually reproduce by random chance all the books in the British Museum. While theoretically possible, picture this scenario: Monkeys are tasked with typing the word "banana" on typewriters with fifty keys. If they press keys at random, and each key has an equal chance of being pressed, the chance that the first six letters pressed spell banana is $(1/50)^6$ (one in fifteen trillion six hundred twenty-five billion). Thus, the probability of having the monkeys type banana is more than zero, but it would be luck, indeed, to have it happen even if they tried all day, every day, for the rest of their natural lives.

By the time monkeys start trying to re-create the complete works of William Shakespeare without errors, assuming the secret to immortality has been discovered and applied to the monkeys, they would probably be hard at work at the end of the universe. To drive the point home, someone actually performed an experiment in which a computer keyboard was left in an enclosure of six Celebes crested macaques in Paignton Zoo in England. Over the course of a month in 2003, the monkeys produced about five pages of writing that largely consisted of the letter "S."

Thankfully, computers are better than monkeys at this sort of work, yet even the most powerful computers are limited when dealing with sufficiently large numbers. Checkers has fairly simple rules but a staggering number of possible moves – some 10^{34} possibilities. It is hard to think about numbers that large, but computer scientist Jonathan Schaeffer compares it to draining the Pacific Ocean and refilling it with an eight-ounce cup, one scoop at a time. Schaeffer spent decades developing an AI called Chinook that eventually solved checkers in 2007. Chess is more complex, having about 10^{120} possible board configurations, which puts a solution beyond the limits of feasible technology. Deep Blue, for example, could only generate every possible move for the next eight moves, and both checkers and chess are nothing like Go, which has 10^{172} possible board configurations. While brute-force computation can work very well with problems that have a limited number of possible solutions, it is less useful for others.

Connectionist AI

Connectionist systems generate intelligent behavior by representing rules in interconnected networks of simple and even uniform units such as artificial neurons. Many of the most dramatic advances achieved by AI in recent years have come from improvements in connectionist techniques such as machine learning, artificial neural networks, and deep learning. Machine learning allows computers to learn from examples and generate their own rules, which may be more accurate than rules explicitly created by programmers, particularly where the rules are based on large datasets and complex patterns that are difficult for people to directly interpret.

Artificial neural networks, one set of algorithms used in machine learning, are inspired by the architecture of the human brain. Each person's brain has about 90 billion individual neurons, which are interconnected in highly complex networks with perhaps hundreds of trillions of connections. These connections change dynamically, or the strength of them changes, as a result of learning and experience. Similarly, artificial neural networks consist of groups of interconnected layers of algorithms that feed data into each other and that can be trained to complete tasks by altering the relevance of data as they pass between layers. During training, the weights attached to different inputs change until the network produces a desired output, at which point the network has developed the ability to complete a task. Deep learning involves many layers of neural networks, and has been responsible for many of the recent advances in speech recognition and computer vision.

Connectionist AI was a focus of development efforts on-and-off throughout the twentieth century, but its utility has dramatically improved in the past decade. In 2011, Jeff Dean and Andrew Ng built a large neural net across 16,000 of Google's server processors and fed it 10 million unlabeled YouTube images. The network spent three days processing the data and taught itself to recognize human faces, human bodies, and cats with accuracy rates of about 75 to 82 percent.[14] The same learning method was then able to substantially outperform other AI systems at a major image recognition contest called the ImageNet Challenge in which programs compete to correctly classify and detect classes of objects and scenes.

This was a breakthrough in machine learning and the start of the Google Brain project. The following year, two graduate students, Alex Krizhevsky and Ilya Sutskever, working at University of Toronto with Geoffrey Hinton built a neural network model called AlexNet, which dominated the ImageNet contest by a margin of more than 10 percent.[15] Google hired all three researchers. Machine learning now plays a major role in a wide variety of Alphabet and Google technologies. For instance, AlphaGo utilizes neural networks.

Advances in AI and Their Applications

AI's increased capabilities are largely due to three parallel developments: more advanced software, greater computing power, and growth of big data. These advances are moving – and have moved – quickly, with improvements taking less and less time with each AI incarnation. Deep Blue, which awed programmers and laypersons alike in 1997, has been retired, but the machine was ten million times faster than the first machine used to play chess in 1951 and was capable of evaluating more than 200 million moves per second. A Samsung Galaxy S10 smartphone is fifty times faster than Deep Blue. Likewise, the modern iPhone has around 100,000 times more processing power than the Apollo 11 computer that put Neil Armstrong and Buzz Aldrin on the moon in 1969, and it holds millions of times more memory.

In 2017, the International Data Corporation forecasted that the "global data-sphere" will include 163 zettabytes of information by 2025, which is more than ten times the 16.1 zettabytes of data available in 2016. It is difficult to conceptualize data on that scale: 163 zettabytes are roughly equivalent to sixteen million years of high-definition video or twenty billion US Libraries of Congress. Big data are critically important for AI, and vice versa. AI can deal with large and complex datasets in ways that people cannot. Big data also can be used to train some forms of AI to progressively improve their performance without explicit programming. The importance of data for AI and other purposes has led to data's being called the new oil or the oil of the twenty-first century (an occasionally criticized metaphor). As the European Commission noted in 2018, "Data is the raw material for most AI technologies."[16]

All big data are not created equal, however, and "garbage in, garbage out" is a maxim in the AI community. For big data to have value for AI, the right kinds of data need to be collected, aggregated, and appropriately utilized. Take the example of an AI's analyzing health care insurer electronic health records to determine if a pharmaceutical medication has adverse events. The AI might need data on exposures (with dates), outcomes, and other health conditions together with insurer enrollment and demographic information, and it might be helpful to link datasets across different time points and insurers. Failure to obtain comprehensive and accurate data used for AI input might result in an incorrect AI output, or if the input is used to train an AI, it might result in an inaccurately biased AI.

Even if the necessary data exist, they still need to be brought together and appropriately translated for AI. Most AI systems are unable to work with unstructured data, which are generally distinguished from structured data by their degree of organization. Structured data usually exist in relational databases where they are categorized and sorted into distinct, easily searchable fields. Unstructured data, by contrast, do not have a predefined data model. They may exist as a heterogenous free-form mix of text, audio, video, and social media postings that have not been labeled or sorted. Most big data now are unstructured, and significant cost and effort are needed to structure them.

AI has enjoyed recent advances in a variety of areas such as computer vision, which deals with how machines can gain a high-level understanding from images or videos, essentially automating the human visual system. In 2015, Microsoft announced it had beat the ImageNet Challenge's dedicated human labeler by classifying more than 95 percent of the images correctly.[17] In 2017, twenty-nine of the thirty-eight competing teams classified more than 95 percent of them correctly.[18] These improvements have translated to practical gains as well. For instance, Facebook's image recognition technology now identifies people, objects, expressions, activities, events, and spaces. This AI has a very rich source of training data – more than two billion photos are uploaded daily to Facebook and platforms it owns: Instagram, WhatsApp, and Messenger. These are impressive achievements, though machines still struggle with visual identification in many situations that are no challenge to people.

AI has made similar advances in natural-language processing to which anyone who uses programs like Siri, Alexa, or Cortana can attest. The idea of machine translation as well as predictions that fully realized machine translation would exist within a few years has been around since the 1950s. Those predictions were unrealistic, but today's machine translation has come a long way. Google Translate, for instance, supports more than a hundred languages, including many by photo, voice, and even real-time video. The Google Translate app is used by more than 500 million people and translates around 143 billion words daily.[19]

To take another example, Microsoft announced in 2017 that its speech recognition system performed as well as human transcribers in recognizing speech from Switchboard Corpus, a collection of thousands of recorded random conversations. Fifteen years before that, machine translation word-error rates hovered around 20 to 30 percent. In 2017, Microsoft's technology reached an error rate of 5.9 percent, the same as a human transcriber.

AI has already had a substantial economic impact and has the potential to have far more, though it is difficult to compare estimates because they often use different definitions of AI.[20] A study by PricewaterhouseCoopers suggests that AI could contribute $15.7 trillion to the global economy in 2030, of which $6.6 trillion could come from increased productivity and $9.1 trillion from consumption-side effects.[21] A report by the McKinsey Global Institute claims the disruptions caused by new technologies such as AI will "happ[en] ten times faster and at 300 times the scale, or roughly 3,000 times the impact" of the Industrial Revolution.[22]

5 AI CHARACTERISTICS

Understanding AI is important for thinking about how it should be regulated and how it challenges existing legal systems. While a conventional machine could exhibit some or all the following characteristics – directly causing physical changes or behaving with limited predictability or explainability – AI is far more likely to display these characteristics and to a greater extent. A difference in degree along one or several of these axes makes AI worth considering as a distinctive phenomenon.

Limited Explainability

An AI's actions cannot always be explained. It may be possible to determine what an AI has done but not how or why it acted as it did. For instance, an algorithm may decline a job application but be unable to articulate why the application was rejected. This lack of explainability is particularly likely in the case of connectionist AI that learns from data. Even if theoretically possible to explain an AI outcome, it may be impracticable given the complexity of AI, the possible resource-intensive nature of such inquiries, and the need to maintain earlier versions of AI and specific data.

Specific vs. General and Weak vs. Strong AI

While AI can already outperform people in breathtaking fashion in some domains, such as board games, in other domains AI is not that useful. All AI is designed to perform narrow or specific tasks – not general ones. For instance, DeepMind's AI can beat the world's best human player at Go, but it cannot translate English to French without being programmed to do so. By contrast, the holy grail of computer science research is developing general AI that can perform any task that a person can perform. But, general and even superintelligent AI are still considered "weak" compared to the self-aware, conscious, and sentient AI that is common in science fiction. This latter sort – "strong" AI – is portrayed as having humanlike abilities to cognitively reason and be morally culpable for its actions. As of today, the prospect of such machines is still safely within the realm of science fiction.

Lack of Predictability

AI can engage in activities that its original programmers may not have intended. Microsoft's chatbot Tay is sometimes invoked as an example of an AI's acting unpredictably. Tay was touted as an experiment in "conversational understanding," an AI that would get smarter through engagement with people. Soon after the bot's launch on social media sites like Twitter, people barraged Tay with misogynistic, racist, and political vitriol – and Tay responded in kind. For instance, when one user asked, "Is Ricky Gervais an atheist?," Tay replied, "ricky gervais learned totalitarianism from adolf hitler, the inventor of atheism."[23] Microsoft discontinued Tay within twenty-four hours. While the specific tweet may have been unforeseeable, in retrospect it is surprising that one of the world's largest technology companies would have so little insight into the nature of online discourse. On the other hand, hindsight is 20/20 and a Chinese predecessor of Tay named Xiaoice reportedly engaged in more than forty million conversations without major incident.[24]

Physicality

Although Tay's activities were entirely digital and limited to the Twittersphere, AI does have the potential to directly cause physical changes when it is embodied in or controls hardware, as in the case of a robot. The first reported robot fatality occurred on the fifty-eighth anniversary of *R.U.R.*'s premiere. In 1979, Robert William, a Ford assembly worker, was killed when a robot's arm struck him in the head. In subsequent litigation, a jury found this accident was due to a lack of safety measures and awarded William's estate $10 million in damages. Of course, it is not necessary for AI to control a robot to cause physical change. An entirely digital AI that exists only on the cloud, an interconnected network of remote servers, could stop someone's pacemaker or target a person for unwanted attention by law enforcement.

Autonomy

Perhaps the most important characteristic of AI from the perspective of AI legal neutrality is its ability to act autonomously – functionally determining for itself how to complete a given task. This characteristic is well illustrated by "The DAO," the most famous attempt to create a decentralized autonomous organization (DAO). The idea was that an entity (organization) would be created on a blockchain, a type of distributed ledger technology (decentralized) used to support cryptocurrencies like Bitcoin. Once set in motion, it would act automatically according to smart contracts (autonomous), which are preprogrammed rules dictating future behavior. In other words, The DAO was an AI that would function independently of its original developers while simultaneously existing across countless computers.

Built by German company Slock.it (and its founders) and launched on the Ethereum blockchain, which generates a cryptocurrency called "Ether," The DAO was meant to operate like a venture capital fund. During a creation period, investors could fund The DAO by purchasing "tokens" using Ether, much like buying shares in a corporation, after which anyone could pitch an investment opportunity that The DAO could fund based on the votes of token holders who, like shareholders in a traditional company, would then receive rewards from profitable projects.

The DAO's code was open-source and made publicly available to anyone to inspect how the program would operate. The primary benefit of this structure is that The DAO's creators would be unable to misappropriate The DAO's funds or misuse the entity. Because it was a technologically cutting-edge project, and it removed the need to trust other people, The DAO was appealing to a particular sort of investor, many of whom were cryptocurrency enthusiasts. In 2016, The DAO resulted in the then-largest crowdfund in history, raising around $150 million worth of Ether.

Unfortunately, before any projects could be funded, a hacker exploited a bug in The DAO's programming and started to withdraw its funds. The same "unstoppable" or "unalterable" architecture that investors were attracted to, which prevented The DAO's creators from changing its code for their own benefit, meant they could not fix the faulty code or directly recover the stolen funds. Stopping the hacker required extreme measures from the Ethereum community. A "hard fork" was instituted, which changed the underlying blockchain protocol's code and resulted in new and old versions of Ethereum: Ethereum and Ethereum Classic. The new blockchain was maintained by those who supported the intervention, and the legacy blockchain was preserved by those who believed the blockchain should be "immutable" and that contributors to The DAO had only themselves to blame.

In the post–hard fork Ethereum blockchain, users who contributed Ether to The DAO were permitted to withdraw their funds. The hacker, meanwhile, was able to withdraw the funds on the significantly less valuable Ethereum Classic blockchain. The decision to hard fork was controversial in the Ethereum community and significantly reduced the value of the Ethereum blockchain. The hacker was never identified, and no civil or criminal charges were levied against The DAO's creators. The US Securities and Exchange Commission investigated The DAO and reported that its tokens were securities and subject to federal securities laws, which appeared to have been violated.

Ultimately, The DAO did not survive this controversy. However, new DAOs are being created. In 2018, the government of Malta considered legislation that would provide legal personality to DAOs.

Further Thoughts

AI has already accomplished feats that critics in previous generations considered impossible. If these developments appear unimpressive today, it is only because problems stop seeming so mysterious once they can be solved. Meanwhile, AI with ever-improving capabilities is being integrated into our daily lives and automating activities that once required significant human effort. While difficult to predict the exact trajectory of AI's continued development, it is self-evident that AI is poised to take over a growing range of activities that were once the exclusive province of people. AI's potential seems virtually unlimited, so the question might not be where AI is headed but when will it get there.

2

Should Artificial Intelligence Pay Taxes?

I regard it as the major domestic challenge, really, of the sixties, to maintain full employment at a time when automation, of course, is replacing men.

– President John F. Kennedy

One of the biggest concerns about AI is the prospect of automation's leading to increased unemployment. This is a concern for good reason. AI can already automate many work functions, and its cost is decreasing at a time when human labor costs are increasing. A number of experts are predicting significant job losses and worsening income inequality as AI continues to improve, and policymakers are actively debating how to deal with technological unemployment, with most proposals focusing on investing in education to train workers in new job types or in social benefits to distribute the gains of automation.

What has yet to be appreciated is that legal standards exacerbate technological unemployment by unintentionally subsidizing automation. Businesses pay less in taxes by having an AI, as well as automation technologies more generally, do the same work as a person. Employers save money by automating, but the government may lose a substantial amount of tax revenue as a result. In the aggregate, automation may cost the US government hundreds of billions of dollars a year – or more.[1]

AI legal neutrality suggests that existing tax policies should change to be at least neutral between AI and human workers and that automation should not be allowed to reduce tax revenue. Neutrality could be achieved by eliminating the preferential treatment provided to AI or by creating offsetting benefits for human laborers. This could be accomplished in a variety of ways, but the best option may be to eliminate taxes on workers such as payroll taxes. This would help AI and people compete on their own merits without taking tax into account, reduce tax complexity, and decrease the taxation of socially valuable labor.

However, it would also dramatically reduce tax revenue. Increasing other types of taxes such as income, consumption (e.g., sales tax), and property could offset this to ensure adequate revenue. This may naturally be a more progressive system, but it could be made deliberately more so by having higher taxes for high earners, luxury goods, and higher-value properties. More ambitiously, capital gains and corporate tax rates could be raised, but any of these measures would help to ensure that the financial benefits of automation are shared without restricting automation when it is genuinely more efficient.

This chapter – divided into three sections – aims to rethink the current tax framework in light of the principle of AI legal neutrality. To begin, the first section provides the background on the costs and benefits of automation and reviews historical concerns about, and efforts to address, technological unemployment. Section 2 delves into an underexplored aspect of automation – that is, tax policy unintentionally favors AI over people – and explains how and why that is the case. Finally, Section 3 proposes ways to apply a principle of AI legal neutrality to tax policy to ensure both effective competition and fiscal solvency.

1 AUTOMATION AND TECHNOLOGICAL UNEMPLOYMENT

History of the Automation Scare

Modern fears of the consequences of automation have been expressed since the Industrial Revolution. In 1772, the writer Thomas Mortimer objected to machines "which are intended almost totally to exclude the labor of the human race."[2] In 1821, the economist David Ricardo argued that automation would result in inequality and that "substitution of machinery for human labour is often very injurious to the interests of the class of labourers .... [It] may render the population redundant and deteriorate the condition of the labourer."[3] In 1839, the philosopher Thomas Carlyle more poetically wrote,

> "The huge demon of Mechanism smokes and thunders, panting as his great task, in all
> sections of English land; changing his *shape* like a very Proteus; and infallibly, at every
> change of shape, *oversetting* whole multitudes of workmen, as if with the waving of his
> shadow from afar, hurling them asunder, this way and that, in their crowded march and
> course of work or traffic; so that the wisest no longer knows his whereabout[s]."[4]

The Industrial Revolution, coupled with these concerns, even gave birth to a social movement that protested the use of new technologies. The Luddites were primarily English textile workers who objected to working conditions in the nineteenth century, and they believed that automation threatened their livelihoods and were opposed to the introduction of industrial machinery. Some Luddites engaged in violent episodes of machine-breaking, in response to which the English government made machine-breaking a capital offense. The Luddite movement died out, but automation concerns persisted throughout the twentieth century, often flaring during times of rapid technological progress. For instance, the debate was revitalized in the 1950s and 1960s with the widespread introduction of office computers and factory robots. In his 1960 election campaign, John F. Kennedy suggested that automation offered "hope of a new prosperity for labor and a new abundance for America," but also that it "carrie[d] the dark menace of industrial dislocation, increasing unemployment, and deepening poverty."[5]

Despite these concerns, technological advances have generally resulted in overall job creation. The computer eliminated jobs but created jobs for working with information created by computers. The automobile eliminated jobs but opened up jobs in the hospitality and food service industries. The tractor and other agricultural advances eliminated jobs but drove job growth in other areas of the economy. Even as agricultural-based employment and agriculture's relative contribution to the gross domestic product (GDP) decreased during the twentieth century, the productivity of farmworkers and agriculture's absolute contribution to GDP increased. Indeed, in each previous era when concerns have been expressed about automation causing mass unemployment, the new technology has created more jobs than it destroyed.

Will History Repeat Itself?

Another period of vigorous public debate about automation and technological unemployment due to recent advances in AI is upon us. Once more, prognosticators are divided into two camps: optimists who claim there will be a net creation of jobs, and pessimists who predict mass unemployment and growing inequality. History favors the optimists. They argue that technological advances will generate widespread benefits and overall job creation, current unemployment may relate more to globalization and offshoring than to technology, and any future technological unemployment would be "only a temporary phase of maladjustment."[6] However, there is reason to think that this time may be different because of AI's growing capabilities.

In 2013, Carl Benedikt Frey and Michael Osborn published an influential study claiming that 47 percent of American jobs are at high risk of automation by the mid-2030s.[7] More recently, Oxford Economics has argued that up to 20 million manufacturing jobs worldwide will be lost to automation by 2030.[8] Forrester predicts job losses of 29 percent by 2030 and 13 percent job creation.[9] Bank of America claims that by 2025, AI may eliminate $9 trillion in employment costs by automating knowledge work.[10] On the other hand, there is also no shortage of optimistic research. For instance, the McKinsey Global Institute argues that while there will be significant job losses due to automation, there will be net positive job growth in the United States through 2030.[11]

While optimists and pessimists disagree about automation's effects on long-term unemployment, both agree it causes short-term job losses and industry-specific disruption. During past episodes of widespread automation and technological change, it took decades to develop new worker skill sets on a significant scale and to build new job markets. Although the Industrial Revolution ultimately resulted in net job creation, it also resulted in periods of mass unemployment and human suffering. Today, regardless of whether there will be detrimental long-term effects, there will almost certainly be significant short-term disruptions.

The Good, Bad, and Ugly of Automation

Automation can create jobs and increase productivity. It can also free up capital for investments in new enterprises, result in the creation of new job types and products, and decrease production costs for existing products. Technological advances have historically upgraded the labor force: Automation has reduced the need for unskilled workers but increased the need for skilled workers. Partly due to technological advances and automation, the United States' GDP has steadily risen from $712 billion in 1965 to $20.5 trillion in 2018. Despite academic criticism, GDP has remained the dominant economic indicator of welfare and standard of living for half a century.

Yet, automation generates wealth unevenly – at times at a someone's expense. In the last twenty-five years, the income share of the top 0.1 percent has increased substantially such that the top 0.1 percent of the US population is now worth about as much as the bottom 90 percent. CEO-to-worker pay ratios have increased a thousandfold since 1950, but overall wages have been stagnant for thirty-five years. AI and automation have contributed to these trends and are likely to accelerate them. The White House Council of Economic Advisors predicts that future automation will disproportionately affect lower-wage jobs and less educated workers, causing greater economic inequality and worsening employment, the combination of which is a recipe for social unrest. As Stephen Hawking warned,

> "Everyone can enjoy a life of luxurious leisure if the machine-produced wealth is shared, or most people can end up miserably poor if the machine-owners successfully lobby against wealth redistribution. So far, the trend seems to be toward the second option, with technology driving ever-increasing inequality."[12]

If workers rendered technologically unemployed are able to transition to new jobs, as has been the case during previous eras of rapid change, labor markets will still experience significant short-term disruptions. That is a best-case scenario, but many experts predict that today's technological advances are fundamentally different from those of the past and large-scale permanent increases in unemployment are inevitable.[13] For example, in 1990 the three largest companies in Detroit with a combined market capitalization of $36 billion employed 1.2 million workers. In 2014, the three largest companies in Silicon Valley with a combined market capitalization of $1.09 trillion employed 137,000 workers.

So automation can contribute to unemployment and inequality, but one of automation's most pronounced, and unappreciated, effects relates to taxes. Automation may substantially reduce tax revenue, even while generating more wealth, because most of the US government's tax revenue comes from taxes on labor. In 2018, the Internal Revenue Service (IRS) reported that more than half of its nearly $3.5 trillion in net collections came from individual income taxes. The next largest source of revenue was employment taxes (largely Medicare, Medicaid, and social security taxes), which contributed more than a trillion dollars. Less than a tenth of revenue comes from business income taxes, and a far smaller amount from excise taxes (taxes on specific goods and activities) and gift and estate taxes. In other words, most revenue comes from taxes – direct and indirect – levied on income and wages by various levels of government, as opposed to business, excise, and gift and estate taxes. The government loses out on employee and employer wage taxes when businesses replace their workers with AI. Even if automation results in greater profitability for a business, a relatively small portion of that profit is remitted in taxes.

Automation Social Policy

Policymakers should act to accommodate and even encourage advances that promote economic value, but it is also important to ensure this value is distributed in a socially just manner. In the middle of the Industrial Revolution, philosopher John Stuart Mill wrote that while automation would ultimately benefit laborers,

> [t]his does not discharge governments from the obligation of alleviating, and if possible preventing, the evils of which this source of ultimate benefit is or may be productive to an existing generation [and] there cannot be a more legitimate object of the legislator's care than the interests of those who are thus sacrificed to the gains of their fellow-citizens and of posterity.[14]

Or, as the US National Science and Technology Council Committee on Technology has argued, "Public policy can address [technological unemployment], ensuring that workers are retrained and able to succeed in occupations that are complementary to, rather than competing with, automation. Public policy can also ensure that the economic benefits created by AI are shared broadly and assure that AI responsibly ushers in a new age in the global economy."[15]

Efforts to alleviate the harms and share the benefits of automation have focused on education and social benefits. In terms of the former, it is thought that technologically unemployed workers need retraining to transition to new job types. President Kennedy's solution was to pass the nation's first and most sweeping federal training program: the Manpower Development and Training Act of 1962. More recently, President Barack Obama provided billions of dollars to fund worker training in part to address technological unemployment. He also proposed a plan to make two years of community college available at no cost for "responsible students" in his 2015 State of the Union Address, although this proposal was never adopted.

Obama's efforts to address AI and automation saw the Executive Office of the President issue a report in 2016 that outlines a three-pronged policy response:

namely, to invest in AI, educate and train Americans for future jobs, and transition workers to ensure widespread benefits. The report advocates strengthening the social safety net through greater investments in programs such as unemployment insurance and Medicaid, proposes the creation of new programs for wage insurance and emergency aid, and argues for building a twenty-first-century retirement system, expanding health care access, and increasing worker bargaining power.

Revitalized concerns about technological unemployment have breathed new life into an old social benefit proposal: basic income, a system of unconditional income to every citizen. There are many ways a basic income could be implemented, sometimes called guaranteed minimum income or universal basic income depending on how it is structured, but the fundamental premise is that the government would provide a fixed amount of money to its citizens regardless of their situation. Some version of basic income has been trialed numerous times on a relatively small scale, with mixed results. The most famous US basic income program is the Alaska Permanent Fund Dividend, which has been unconditionally paying state residents since 1982. In 2018, Alaskan residents received $1,600 for the year.

More recently, from 2017 to 2019, Finland ran a pilot program to give about $600 per month to 2,000 unemployed citizens, with no other requirements. The program cost around $23 million in total. The final results of the study are not yet available, but preliminary evidence suggests it had no impact on employment but improved participant health and well-being.[16] The Finnish government, which initially considered replacing earnings-based insurance benefits with a basic income, has declined to continue and expand the trial.

Proponents of basic income, like Mark Zuckerberg and Elon Musk, argue it will reduce unemployment, poverty, and disincentives for the unemployed to work (as under conventional unemployment schemes recipients generally lose their unemployment benefits after returning to work). It might also encourage education by providing support for a period of training. Critics argue that a guaranteed minimum income will encourage recipients to remain unemployed and discourage additional education. Y Combinator, the famous Silicon Valley start-up incubator, is planning a randomized controlled trial to evaluate the effects of basic income across two US states.

Efforts to provide basic income coming from places like Finland and Silicon Valley might not be surprising, but in 1969 President Richard Nixon planned an even more ambitious basic income. His Family Assistance Plan (FAP) initially would have provided an unconditional income of around $1,600 (around $11,000 in 2019) a year to a family of four living in poverty. An unconditional basic income had just been meticulously trialed on around 8,500 Americans without evidence it resulted in decreased work or that it was prohibitively expensive.

On the day Nixon intended to announce the FAP, his advisors presented him with a report of a trial of basic income from early nineteenth-century England known as the Speenhamland system. His advisors claimed the trial was a colossal disaster on the basis of a 150-year-old English Royal Commission report based on faulty science. Nixon's advisors then persuaded him that the FAP would not only threaten capitalism but also pauperize the masses and trap them in a cycle of vicious poverty. In response, Nixon decided to transform FAP from a "welfare" plan to a "workfare" plan that would require all recipients other than mothers with young children to work, but even that was never enacted. Democrats felt the level of basic income was not sufficient, and Republicans, many of whom initially supported the proposal, soon turned against it. Lobbying for workfare helped turn conservatives against basic income as well as the idea of America as a "welfare state."

Improving education and social benefit systems will not be easy. In the abstract most policymakers agree on the desirability of bettering worker training as it will enlarge the productive labor force, but "delivering this education and training will require significant investments."[7] The social benefit system will also entail more investment, but it faces an additional hurdle: a lack of consensus that enhanced benefits are a desirable aim. In any event, the fact that automation creates a need for greater government investment is well-known.

What has so far been largely ignored in the automation debate is that automation will make it more difficult for the government to make these investments if tax revenues are reduced. As a very rough estimate, revenue loss can be estimated by multiplying an effective tax rate by the gross salary loss due to automation. In January 2017, the McKinsey Global Institute claimed that about half of current work activities could be automated using currently demonstrated technologies, which would eliminate $2.7 trillion in annual wages just in the United States.[18] Workers pay high effective tax rates ranging from 25 to 55 percent when all tax types are taken into account. This suggests that worker automation could result in hundreds of billions, or even trillions, of dollars lost per year in tax revenue at various levels of government. Tax is thus critically important to the automation debate. Tax policies should not encourage automation, unless it is part of a deliberate strategy based on sound public policy.

While there has been a lively public discourse on technological unemployment and income disparity, the automation debate has historically ignored the issue of taxation, and this has only recently started to change. In February 2017, the European Parliament rejected a proposal to impose a "robot tax" on owners to fund support for displaced workers, citing concerns of stifling innovation. The next day, Bill Gates stated that he thought governments should tax companies' use of robots to slow the spread of automation and fund other types of employment. Former US Secretary of the Treasury Lawrence Summers then claimed Gates' argument was "profoundly misguided." In August 2017, South Korea announced plans for the world's first "tax on robots" by limiting tax incentives for automated machines. Previously, Korean businesses were able to deduct 3 to 7 percent of an investment in automation equipment from their corporate tax, depending on the size of their operation. The reform decreased the deduction rate by up to 2 percent.

2 CURRENT TAX POLICIES FAVOR AUTOMATION AND REDUCE TAX REVENUE

Consider an AI that could automate the job of a diagnostic radiologist (a doctor who evaluates images like X-ray, MRI, and CT scans), or it could make other radiologists so efficient that a hospital would need one less radiologist. This might be the case if the AI could only perform certain tasks that a human radiologist could do, such as review chest X-rays for pneumonia. Without the need for someone to perform this task, the remaining radiologists on staff could focus on tasks that the AI cannot perform. Even if the AI only does an initial review of an image, still requiring that a human physician confirm its analysis, the AI is making the doctor more productive (i.e., faster), and it may then result in less need for a doctor.

On a pretax basis, over four years, the outlay for this AI, which includes money spent to acquire, maintain, repair, and upgrade fixed or capital assets such as machines or intangible assets like (some) software, together with the costs for operating the AI (electricity, etc.), might be $2.1 million. The wages and other costs (healthcare, retirement funding, etc.) associated with a human radiologist might be $2 million over the same period. However, the AI might be associated with tax benefits that do not apply to the doctor and reduce its cost to $1.9 million. A business using a rational cost-based decision model would choose to automate.

The tax system is not neutral between work performed by AI and people. Automation provides several tax advantages. Businesses that automate can avoid employee and employer wage taxes. In the United States, an employer and employee pay matching amounts totaling 12.4 percent of an employee's salary, matching Medicare payments totaling 2.9 percent (applied on the first $127,200 of earnings), and an additional 0.9 percent Medicare surcharge (applied on earnings over $200,000). Employers can also claim accelerated tax depreciation on capital costs for automated workers.[19] Tax depreciation refers here to the deduction (a reduction in the tax base) claimed by a business with respect to capital outlay for automated workers. Deductions for capital outlays for automation equipment will allow a business to reduce its tax base over time, which reduces the amount of tax that is payable. Of course, wages paid to individuals are also tax deductible, but the timing of the deduction may work differently for AI than it does for people and may have a significant effect on a business' tax burden.

An accelerated tax deduction means that the deduction may be claimed earlier than its actual economic depreciation (the reduction in the value of an asset over time). For example, assume an industrial robot has a total capital cost of $100,000 and seven years of useful life, while an employee has a total wage cost of $100,000 over seven years. If accelerated depreciation for capital is available, the business might be able to claim a large portion of the $100,000 depreciation as a tax deduction in year one rather than pro-rata over seven years. The business might claim tax depreciation for an automated worker of $50,000 in year one, $30,000 in year two, $10,000 in year three, and in diminishing amounts to year seven.

By contrast, wage taxes must be deducted as paid (i.e., one-seventh in each year). In this case, a present value benefit will accrue from claiming accelerated tax deductions for automated workers relative to deductions for employee wages, even when the $100,000 capital outlay is paid up-front. This is possible because many large businesses have significant amounts of free cash in reserve that is not paid out to shareholders to limit tax liability.[20] The present value of the accelerated tax deduction on capital investment is greater than the discounted value of the return a business could make by investing this free cash held on its balance sheet. The situation may be different where AI is considered an intangible asset rather than a tangible asset. Some, but not all, software is considered an intangible asset and there may be some complex rules about the timing of deductions. Generally, tangible assets are depreciated whereas intangible assets are amortized. As a rule, amortization is more difficult to accelerate than depreciation.

Tax depreciation (whether accelerated or not) is also generally available even when the actual rate of inflation is equal to or greater than the economic depreciation. Inflation here refers to the rate at which the general level of prices for goods and services is rising such that it would cost more to build the same machine next year than it would cost today. The issue becomes significant when, as in the example, it is presumed for tax purposes that the robot will wear out after seven years, but it turns out to actually increase in nominal value rather than decrease. This will only sometimes be the case with AI per se, as software is often quickly rendered obsolete, but it may be more likely with industrial machinery capable of automation.

Where AI does increase in nominal value over time, an incremental tax benefit accrues where the rate of inflation is higher than the rate of the actual diminishment in economic value and the nominal (or inflationary) difference is never recaptured in the tax system. In the corporate setting, this recapture of tax book to inflation difference would only accrue on the disposal of the asset, which rarely occurs. The same principle applies to commercial real estate, where tax depreciation is allowable on an asset that is actually increasing (not decreasing) in nominal value over time, and the difference is not adjusted for tax purposes.

Businesses can also use accounting tricks to report a tax benefit to earnings due to automation, which businesses might want to do for a variety of reasons, such as making the company look more attractive to potential investors. Where tax depreciation is accelerated relative to book depreciation (the amount reported on financial statements), a business may generally claim a profit (or earnings benefit) to reported earnings from the tax benefit. Thus, a large corporation enjoys a book benefit to reported financial earnings from the differential in depreciation periods. Any business seeking to accelerate reported earnings could use automation to achieve such a timing benefit.

Finally, indirect taxes also encourage businesses to automate. Indirect taxation refers to taxes levied on goods and services rather than on profits; the primary examples are the retail sales tax (RST) levied by states and municipalities in the United States and VAT in most other countries. Employers are thought to bear some of the incidence of indirect tax, as worker salaries and retirement benefits must be increased proportionately to offset the indirect tax. In the case of automated workers, however, the burden of indirect taxes is entirely avoided by a business because it does not need to provide for an AI's consumption. In general, business expenditures for capital assets are exempt from indirect taxation or yield a deduction for RST or VAT.

Automation Reduces Tax Revenue

The share of the tax base borne by labor is increasing. For 2018, the IRS reported that out of nearly $3.5 trillion in net collections, individual income taxes accounted for 56.9 percent, employment taxes 32.7 percent, business income taxes 7.6 percent, excise taxes 2.1 percent, and estate and gift taxes 0.7 percent.[21] In the European Union, high rates of wage taxation are levied in addition to VAT, which is also thought to burden workers in their role as consumers. Moreover, capital taxation is trending sharply downward in nearly all jurisdictions. Corporate taxation now comprises roughly one-half of its respective share compared to prior decades.[22] It is decreasing further in light of the Tax Cuts and Jobs Act of 2017, which cut the corporate tax rate from 35 percent to 21 percent in 2018. Likewise, in Europe, lower taxation of capital relative to other types of taxes is welcomed as a means of international tax competition.

Worker taxation is different from corporate taxation in several respects. Tax avoidance planning is not generally available to wage earners. For instance, an employee cannot use transfer pricing techniques to shift earned income into a 0 percent-taxed entity in the Cayman Islands. Also, wage earnings are not subject to potential deferral, meaning labor income is taxed currently whereas capital may be taxed upon future disposition of an asset. Human capital is also not depreciable, so a person may not get a tax deduction for education or medical costs – at least not up to the full amount of the investment.

By contrast, machinery or other equipment yields an immediate and ongoing tax deduction to a business until the equipment's tax basis is reduced to zero. Workers are additionally subject to various forms of indirect taxation, whereas business machinery is often exempted from RST and VAT. If corporate taxes decline as a share of the tax base while the overall level of taxation holds constant, other types of taxation might increase to cover the difference. While a government might choose to increase borrowing or decrease spending, over the long term this will likely have negative economic effects.

3 POLICY OPTIONS FOR AN AUTOMATION TAX

The current tax system is designed to principally tax people, not AI. This creates a situation in which businesses – with all else being equal – are incentivized to automate to save on taxes. A major automation policy issue is therefore how to adjust the tax system to be neutral between AI and people. This could be done through some combination of granting offsetting tax preferences for workers or reducing the tax benefits for using AI. In any event, another major tax challenge that AI presents is how to prevent the possible future automation of significant segments of the labor force from threatening both short- and long-term fiscal solvency.

Leveling the Playing Field

The first way to ensure effective competition between laborers and AI is to grant offsetting tax preferences to human workers. The tax preference for wages could entail a repeal of the employer and employee contributions to the social security and Medicare systems. The result would be that both people and AI would be exempt in terms of wage taxes – not just automated workers. In terms of income taxation, an offsetting preference for human workers could be designed as an accelerated deduction for future wage compensation expenses (i.e., the business would get an accelerated tax deduction) to match the accelerated depreciation for AI.

The second approach could disallow corporate tax deductions for automation. The basic idea is to reverse each of the tax benefits in relation to accelerated deductions, indirect tax benefits and avoiding the levy on wage taxes. The South Korean "robot tax" adopted this strategy in part by reducing deductions for investment in automated machines. Regarding federal income taxation, the disallowance of tax preferences upon some threshold of income level is a common practice in the Internal Revenue Code and is often referred to as a "phaseout," which reduces tax benefits for some taxpayers, such as the child tax credit and certain contributions to retirement accounts. For instance, student loan interest is deductible but not for individuals with more than $80,000 in modified adjusted gross income ($165,000 for joint filers).[23]

Some phaseouts reduce credits, others reduce deductions. A new code provision could be designed with a similar phaseout, where depreciation or other expenses related to automated workers would be disallowed based on a reported level of automation, rather than income. Businesses with high levels of worker layoffs due to automation, or high profit-to-employment ratios, could have their tax depreciation automatically reduced beyond a certain threshold. The Treasury Department would need to craft detailed regulations and criteria to identify the threshold and to measure the level of automation required to trigger the disallowance.

Either increasing workers' benefits or reducing benefits for the use of AI could achieve greater balance between taxing laborers and AI. However, neither approach will adequately address the decline in the wage tax base. Further, granting offsetting tax preferences for human workers would worsen the decline in the wage tax base by, among other things, eliminating around a third of federal tax revenue. This would accelerate the insolvency of the social security system, unless the resultant decrease in tax collections were otherwise offset.

Ensuring Adequate Revenue

With or without a more neutral system, a second tax challenge posed by AI is how to prevent the future automation of large segments of the labor force from threatening fiscal solvency. This could be done by increasing, say, property and sales taxes. Shifting the tax burden from payroll to sales taxes would make it less burdensome for businesses to employ people, and it may be more progressive to generate tax revenue from property and sales taxes than from wage taxes. This would tax capital to a greater extent than labor because individuals and businesses paying sales and property taxes will in part be taxed on income derived from capital investment. More ambitiously, the tax burden on capital could be raised by (1) instituting an automation tax based on technological unemployment, (2) increasing taxes preferentially on companies that are profitable with minimal labor with a "corporate self-employment tax," (3) increasing general corporate tax rates, or (4) increasing other forms of capital taxation.

First, an incremental federal automation tax could be levied to the extent workers are laid off or replaced by machines. Many states use a similar system with respect to unemployment compensation: Worker layoffs are tracked, and employers are given corresponding ratings. They must then pay into an unemployment insurance scheme based on their ratings. So, a business with more layoffs pays more in taxes for unemployment insurance. A similar scheme could be applied to a federal automation tax through the collection of worker layoff data. This information could then be used to levy an additional federal tax to the extent the Treasury Department determines the layoffs were due to automation. A drawback to the levy of an additional automation tax is that it would increase the relative complexity of the tax system and increase compliance costs.

Second, a corporate self-employment tax could be levied for businesses that produce outputs with relatively limited human labor. The additional taxes could be a substitute amount for social security and Medicare wage taxes avoided by businesses with automated labor. In part, this would be the corollary to the individual self-employment tax where a small-business owner is required to pay into the social security system approximating the social security taxes that would be paid on her own wages deemed to be paid to self. This could be based on a ratio of corporate profits to gross employee compensation expense. If the ratio exceeds an amount determined by the Treasury (in reference to industry standards), then backup withholding could apply on corporate profits. The gross amount of the automation tax could be designed to match the wage taxes avoided by businesses with automated workers. A disadvantage, however, of this corporate self-employment tax is that it could penalize businesses that are automating in socially beneficial ways or that have business models that rely on minimal human labor for nontax reasons.

The third option is to increase corporate tax rates either by raising the statutory tax rate above 21 percent or eliminating certain deductions that result in businesses' paying less than the statutory rate. For instance, Congress could end the deductions for pass-through businesses (limited liability companies, partnerships, and S-corps) in the Tax Cuts and Jobs Act of 2017. Those resulted in more than $40 billion in tax breaks just in 2018. Finally, corporate taxes are far from the only kind of taxes on capital. Increasing capital gains taxes, for example, which are assessed on the profits from the sale of an asset, such as land or a business, are another way to raise the relative tax burden on capital. For most assets held for more than a year, the capital gains tax rate is 0, 15, or 20 percent depending on taxable income and filing status. This is significantly below the tax rates for ordinary income (10 to 37 percent). The appeal of a general increase to capital gains and corporate tax rates is that it would not discriminate against certain business models; rather, it would more evenly increase the tax burden on capital versus labor.

The primary concern about increasing capital tax rates is discouraging investment. Investors consider tax rates in deciding how to invest their capital, and higher tax rates can reduce anticipated returns. Taxation of capital has historically been disfavored because capital is thought to be mobile, or at least more mobile than labor, so increasing tax rates might cause capital investments to head to jurisdictions with lower tax rates. The absence of an internationally harmonized tax regime leads to international tax competition and, to some degree, a race to the bottom.[24] This concern is legitimate, but it would also seem to favor every jurisdiction's abolishing all capital taxes, which would likely lead to even greater wealth disparities.

Another school of thought disputes the prevailing narrative around international tax competition and notes that relatively high tax rates do not historically appear to have been a barrier to US-based investments. Investors and businesses need access to large, developed markets like the United States, and relatively high tax rates might be the price of admission. In fact, paradoxically, higher corporate tax rates might encourage capital investments because they can result in tax deductions with greater value. Higher corporate tax rates increase the relative value of tax deductions for marginal investment, where "marginal" investment refers to incremental investment made only because of the tax system. Multinational businesses may make capital investment into higher tax jurisdictions in lieu of tax haven jurisdictions principally to claim tax deductions of relatively higher value. Partly for this reason, for smaller and growing businesses that are reinvesting profits back into their businesses, the higher rate of corporate tax is not a major disincentive because ongoing tax deductions will substantially reduce the tax base regardless of the ultimate tax rate to be applied.

Further Thoughts

Several potential tax policy solutions exist to address the legal imbalance between AI and people and create a more neutral system in which actors will make decisions based on nontax reasons. Tax neutrality, widely accepted as an economically efficient principle for organizing a tax system, is more likely to have fewer negative effects, have lower administration and compliance costs, promote distributional fairness, and increase transparency, thus resulting in a broader tax base with lower rates. Non-neutralities in the tax system distort choices and behavior other than for economic reasons and encourage socially wasteful efforts to reduce tax payments. They can thus "create complexity, encourage avoidance, and add costs for both taxpayers and governments."[25]

The advantage of tax neutrality between people and AI is that it permits the marketplace to adjust without tax distortions. Businesses should then only automate if it will be more efficient without considering taxes. Since the current tax system favors automated workers, a move toward a neutral tax system could increase the appeal of human workers. The increased tax revenue from neutral taxation could then be used to provide improved education and training for workers rendered unemployed by AI. Should the pessimist's prediction of a near future with substantially increased unemployment due to automation manifest, these taxes could support social benefit programs such as basic income. And while it will likely generate more wealth than has ever been possible, automation should not come at the expense of the most vulnerable.

3

Reasonable Robots

I visualize a time when we will be to robots what dogs are to humans, and I'm rooting for the machines.

– Claude Shannon

AI already diagnoses disease, drafts legal contracts, and provides translation services. But what happens when these AI systems cause harm? What happens when a machine fails to diagnose a cancer, writes a faulty agreement, or starts a war? How should the law respond to accidents caused by AI? With an already existing body of law developed to deal with accidents, tort law will play a central role in answering these and other questions. A tort is a harmful civil act, as opposed to a criminal one, other than under contract, where one person is damaged by another, and it gives way to a right to sue. The goals of tort law are many: to reduce accidents, provide a peaceful means of dispute resolution, promote positive social values, and so forth.

Whether tort law is the best means for achieving all these goals is debatable, but jurists are united in considering accident reduction one of the central aims, if not the primary one, of tort law. By creating a framework for shifting the costs of accidents from injured victims to those who caused harm (tortfeasors), tort law deters unsafe conduct. A purely financially motivated rational actor will reduce potentially harmful activity to the extent that the cost of accidents exceeds the benefits of the activity. This liability framework has far-reaching and sometimes complex impacts on behavior. It can either accelerate or impede the introduction of new technologies.

Most injuries caused by people are evaluated under a negligence standard in which liability depends on whether there was unreasonable conduct. This generally requires proof that a defendant acted unreasonably considering foreseeable risks. The standard is premised on what an objective and hypothetical "reasonable" person would have done under the same circumstances. When an AI causes those same injuries, however, a strict liability standard applies. Strict liability is a theory of liability without fault; it applies without regard to whether a defendant's conduct is socially blameworthy. This distinction has financial consequences and a corresponding impact on the rate of technology adoption. It discourages automation because there is a greater risk of liability when an AI performs the same activity as a person. It also means that in cases where automation would improve safety, the current framework to prevent accidents may have the opposite effect.

The principle of AI legal neutrality suggests the solution is to evaluate the acts of AI tortfeasors under a negligence standard, rather than a strict liability standard, in cases where an AI behaves like a human tortfeasor in the traditional negligence paradigm. Liability would be based on an AI's behavior rather than its design, and this would provide added benefit in cases when it would be difficult to prove a design defect due to system complexity or limited explainability. For the purposes of ultimate financial liability, the AI's supplier (e.g., manufacturers and retailers) should still be responsible for satisfying judgments, which is largely the case under standard principles of product liability law.

The most important implication of this line of reasoning is that just as AI tortfeasors should be compared to human tortfeasors, so too should humans be compared to AI. Once AI becomes safer than people and practical to substitute for people, AI should set the baseline for the new standard of care. This means that human defendants would no longer have their liability based on what a hypothetical reasonable person would have done in the situation, but what an AI would have done.

In time, as AI comes to increasingly outperform people, this rule will mean that someone's best efforts would no longer be sufficient to avoid liability. It would not mandate automation in the interests of freedom and autonomy, but people would engage in certain activities at their own peril. Such a rule is consistent with the rationale for the objective standard of the reasonable person, and it would benefit the general welfare. Eventually, the continually improving reasonable robot standard should apply to AI tortfeasors, at which point AI should cause so little harm that the primary effect of the standard would make human tortfeasors essentially strictly liable for their harms.

The remaining chapter, divided into three sections, reconstructs tort law for the time when AI becomes a safer and more practical alternative to humans. Section 1 provides background on injuries caused by machines and how the law has evolved to address these harms. It also discusses the role of tort law in injury prevention and the development of negligence and strict product liability. Section 2 argues that while some forms of automation should prevent accidents, the current tort framework may act as a deterrent to adopting safer technologies. This section proposes a new categorization of AI-generated torts, contends that the acts of AI tortfeasors should be evaluated under a negligence rather than a strict liability standard, and goes on to propose rules for implementing the system. Finally, Section 3 contends that once AI becomes safer than people and automation is practical, the reasonable AI, or the "reasonable robot" in the case of a physically embodied AI, should become the new standard of care. It explains how this standard would function, considers when the standard should apply to AI tortfeasors, and argues the reasonable robot standard works better than the standard of a reasonable person using an AI. At some point, AI will be so safe that the standard's most significant effect would be to internalize the cost of accidents on human tortfeasors.

1 LIABILITY FOR MACHINE INJURIES

A Brief History

For as long as people have used machines, injuries have resulted – and machines have been with us for quite some time. The earliest evidence of simple machines, tools that redirect force to make work easier like pulleys and levers, dates back millions of years to the beginning of the Stone Age. In fact, the Stone Age is so named because it is characterized by the use of stone to make simple machines such as axes. The primary function of these tools was to hunt and cut meat, but they were also used to facilitate violence against people – and no doubt used negligently as well. As the use and complexity of simple machines grew, so too did the resultant injuries: Mesopotamian surgeons botched procedures and Greek construction zones were so dangerous they required that physicians be on-site. Such injuries continued unabated from the time complex machines were invented by the ancient Chinese and Greeks to the time of the first modern industrial machines.

The Industrial Revolution marked a turning point in the role of machines in society. Major technological advances in textiles, transportation, and iron making occurred during this period, and these resulted in the development of machines for shaping materials and the rise of the factory system as well as a dramatic increase in the number and severity of machine injuries. Working in industrial settings was dangerous business, in part because employers often had minimal liability for employee harms. These dangerous working conditions persisted well into the twentieth century before the US government began collecting data on work-related injuries in a systematic way. In 1913, the Bureau of Labor estimated that 23,000 workers died from work-related injuries (albeit an imperfect proxy for machine injuries) out of a workforce of 38 million, a rate of sixty-one deaths per 100,000 workers.[1]

In the modern era, the rate of work-related injuries has declined significantly. In 2017, for example, the Bureau of Labor reported 5,147 fatal work injuries, a rate of 3.5 per 100,000 workers.[2] There are several reasons for this decline: changes to tort liability, evolved societal and ethics norms that place a greater priority on human welfare, a modern system of regulations and criminal liability that protects worker well-being, and improvements in safety technology. Yet, despite significant progress in workplace safety, accidents are still a serious societal concern. Every year, just in the United States, workplace accidents cost around $190 billion and are responsible for about 4,000 deaths. More broadly, unintentional injuries cost around $850 billion and kill more than 150,000 people annually, around 6 percent of all deaths. According to the Centers for Disease Control and Prevention (CDC), unintentional injuries are the third-leading cause of death.

Tort Law as a Mechanism for Accident Prevention

Part of the reason for the decline in workplace injuries is that tort law provides a stronger financial incentive for safer conduct. The law has evolved from a system designed to insulate employers and manufacturers from liability to one with greater regard for worker and consumer health. In its quest to reduce accidents, tort law has far-reaching and sometimes complex impacts on behavior; it can either accelerate the introduction of new technologies, as is the case with the use of glaucoma testing (the obligatory puff of air one has come to expect in an optometrist's office), or discourage the use of new technologies, as is generally the case in medical care, a field in which the standard of care is usually based on customary practice. Torts are typically categorized based on the level of fault they require (or based on the interests they protect). At one end of the spectrum are intentional torts involving intent to harm or malice; on the other are strict liability torts, which do not require fault. Covering the "great mass of cases" in the middle are harms involving negligence.[3]

Negligence

The concept of negligence is the primary theory through which courts deal with accidents and unintended harms. In practice, to prevail in most personal injury cases, a plaintiff (or claimant) must prove by a preponderance of evidence (more likely than not) that the defendant (or respondent) owed the plaintiff a duty of reasonable care, the defendant breached that duty, the breach caused the plaintiff's damages, and the plaintiff suffered compensable damages. This generally requires proof that the defendant acted negligently, which is to say they acted unreasonably considering foreseeable risks. This standard is premised on what an objective and hypothetical reasonable person would do under the same circumstances. Thus, if the courts determine that a reasonable person would not have headed out to sea without a radio (the means by which to receive warnings of inclement weather), manufactured a ginger beer with a snail inside, or dropped heavy objects off the side of a building (all real, and famous, cases involving careless behavior), then these activities could expose a defendant to liability.

Society has interests in sometimes competing values: reducing injuries and compensating victims as well as encouraging economic growth and progress. One way that tort law attempts to achieve a balance is by permitting recovery in negligence, only where there has been socially blameworthy conduct. Thus, where a defendant has acted reasonably, even if the defendant has caused serious injury to a plaintiff, there will generally be no liability. Juries play a key role in determining the reasonable person standard as applied to the facts of a case.

Strict and Product Liability

While negligence governs virtually all accidents, there are exceptions. For instance, defendants may be strictly liable – liable without fault – for harms they cause as a result of certain types of activities like disposing of hazardous waste or using explosives. Thus, a defendant corporation that takes every reasonable care to prevent injury before dusting crops might nevertheless find itself liable for injuries it causes to a bystander. One of the most important modern applications of strict liability is to product liability, which refers to responsibility for the commercial transfer of a product that causes harm because it is defective, or its properties are falsely represented.

Product injuries cause upward of 200 million injuries a year in the United States. In most instances, members of the supply chain (e.g., manufacturers and retailers) are strictly liable for defective products. The bulk of product liability cases involve claims for damages against a manufacturer or retailer by a person injured while using a product. Typically, a plaintiff will try to prove that an injury was the result of some inherent defect of a product or its marketing, and that the product was flawed or falsely advertised. Defendants, in turn, attempt to prove that their products were reasonably designed, properly made, and accurately marketed. Defendants may argue that plaintiff injuries were the result of improper and unforeseeable use of the product, or that something other than the product caused the harm.

Product liability was not always governed by strict liability. Originally, US courts followed the English doctrine of *caveat emptor* (let the buyer beware) for product liability claims, reflecting a national philosophy embracing individualism and free enterprise. Toward the end of the nineteenth century, however, states began increasingly employing the doctrine of *caveat venditor* (let the seller beware) and an implied warranty of merchantable quality. Under this doctrine, "Selling for a sound price raises an implied warranty that the thing sold is free from defects, known and unknown [to the seller]."[4] Yet even so, manufacturers were in large part able to avoid liability for defective products by essentially arguing that they lacked a contract with consumers (privity of contract). This was possible because in most cases consumers purchased products from third-party retailers rather than directly from manufacturers.

This changed in 1916 with the New York Court of Appeals decision in *MacPherson* v. *Buick Motor Co.*, a case involving a motorist who was injured when one of the wooden wheels of his Buick collapsed. He subsequently attempted to sue the manufacturer (Buick) rather than the dealership where he purchased the vehicle. The court, in rejecting a defense based on privity of contact, held that if "the manufacturer of such a foreseeably dangerous product knows that it will be used by persons other than the purchaser, and used without new tests, then, irrespective of contract, the manufacturer of this thing of danger is under a duty to make it carefully."[5] *MacPherson* spurred negligence claims against manufacturers across the country as state courts one-by-one adopted the case's holding. This shift was accompanied by growing public support for consumer protection together with the understanding that liability would not unduly burden economic activity. Businesses are often in the best position to prevent product injuries and can distribute liability through insurance.

In 1963, the Supreme Court of California decided *Greenman* v. *Yuba Power Products Inc.*, which held that manufacturers of defective products are strictly liable for injuries they cause. This case represents the birth of modern products liability law in the United States. After this decision, the doctrine of strict product liability spread rapidly across the nation.

Of course, today's product liability law is not as simple as this brief narrative suggests. It combines tort law (e.g., negligence, strict liability, and deceit), contract law (e.g., warranty), both common and statutory law (e.g., statutory sales law under Article 2 of the Uniform Commercial Code), and a hodgepodge of state "reform" acts. State statutes have attempted to reform products liability law, often to limit the rights of consumers in order to protect manufacturers. For our purposes, however, it suffices to say this: As a general matter, manufacturers and retailers are strictly liable for injuries caused by defective products.

2 AI-GENERATED TORTS

Automation Will Prevent Accidents

On March 18, 2018, an autonomous vehicle (AV) operated by Uber killed a pedestrian in Arizona. The AV, a Volvo XC90 SUV, was in autonomous mode when it struck Elaine Herzberg, who was crossing the street with her bicycle, at around 10 p.m. The AV was equipped with a light detection and ranging system (lidar), which illuminates targets with pulsed laser light and measures the reflected pulses with a sensor. Lidar should reveal objects hundreds of feet away at night as well as during the day. Indeed, Uber's self-driving software detected Herzberg but failed to stop in time. Because the AV was still in testing, Uber had a "backup" driver in the vehicle to take control in the event the software failed. However, the driver was watching *The Voice*, a TV show, on her mobile phone and failed to notice Herzberg in time. For that matter, Herzberg was crossing an unmarked, unlit segment of road at night. There seems to have been plenty of blame to go around, but nothing absolves the AV of failing to stop. This event is the first pedestrian fatality involving an AV, and it is generally considered the first death caused by an AV. Earlier fatalities had occurred with Tesla drivers operating in Autopilot mode, but regulators did not consider the AV at fault in those cases.

Surveys of attitudes toward self-driving cars have produced mixed results but have often uncovered negative opinions. A 2016 survey by the American

Automobile Association reported that three of four US drivers surveyed said they would feel "afraid" to ride in a self-driving car.[6] Only one in five said they would trust a driverless car to drive itself while they were inside. Another survey found that most UK citizens would feel uncomfortable with self-driving vehicles on the road, and more than three-quarters would want to retain a steering wheel.[7] Regulators are more optimistic, but they are still being cautious. Until 2016, California required human drivers be present in all self-driving cars being tested on public roads. Unmanned vehicles can now operate on public roads under certain circumstances.

Yet much of the public discourse on self-driving cars is misguided. The critical issue is not whether AI is perfect (it is not), but whether it is safer than people (it will be). Nearly all crashes, 94 percent, involve human error. A human driver causes a fatality about every 100 million miles, resulting in tremendous human and financial costs. The US Department of Transportation estimates the economic costs of those accidents at more than $240 billion. More than 35,000 people die from motor vehicle accidents each year in the United States, and more than a million die each year worldwide. Someone is killed in a motor vehicle accident on average about once every twenty-five seconds.

By contrast, the Uber fatality was the first known death in hundreds of millions of miles driven by AVs. It is also important to note that driverless technologies are in their infancy, and they will be dramatically improved in a decade. At the point where automated cars are ten times safer than human drivers, that could reduce the annual number of US motor vehicle fatalities to about 3,500. This is the conclusion of a report from the consulting firm McKinsey & Company, which predicts AVs will reduce the number of automobile deaths by about 30,000 a year.[8] However, the report estimates that self-driving technologies will not be adopted widely enough to permit this outcome until the middle of the century.

AVs may be the most prominent and disruptive upcoming example of AI's automating activities with a significant risk of harm, but automation has the potential to improve safety in a variety of settings. For instance, IBM's AI Watson works with clinicians to analyze patient medical records and provide evidence-based cancer treatment options. Like self-driving cars, Watson does not need to be perfect to improve safety – it just needs to be better than people. Medical error is one of the leading causes of death.

Estimates vary, but a 2016 study in the *British Medical Journal* reports that it is the third-leading cause of death in the United States, behind cardiovascular disease and cancer (the CDC ranks unintentional injuries as the third-leading cause of death but does not include medical error in cause of death rankings).[9] Some companies already claim their AI outperforms doctors at certain tasks, and those claims are believable. Why should AI not be able to outperform a person when the AI can access the entire wealth of medical literature with perfect recall, benefit from the experience of directly having treated millions of patients, and be immune to fatigue?

Strict Liability Discourages Automation

To see why the current tort framework discourages automation, let us turn to the question of when it makes economic sense for a business to replace a person with an AI. In practice, it may be complex to calculate the cost of a human driver versus a self-driving vehicle. Human employees have costs in excess of their salaries and wages, such as tax liability, as discussed in Chapter 2, for employer portions of social security tax, Medicare tax, state and federal unemployment tax, and workers' compensation; employer portions of health insurance; paid holidays, vacations, and sick days; and contributions toward retirement, pension, savings, and profit-sharing plans. AI costs may be simpler to estimate, but they are also uncertain. There are likely to be costs associated with repair, maintenance, and operation in addition to purchase or license costs and taxes.

Added to the direct financial costs associated with employing an operator, there may be indirect financial and nonfinancial costs, known and unknown, that guide a decision. For example, a person may require vocational training or be unable to work due to sickness; AI may require software updates or malfunction. Employing human operators may result in greater expenses for legal fees, administrative and overhead costs, and compliance with regulatory and employment requirements. AI may infringe patents or result in negative publicity. Businesses' deciding whether to automate may also consider broader social policies. For instance, they may choose not to automate because of a perception it promotes income inequality and unemployment. But businesses are required to act in the best interests of shareholders, and most interpret this duty as a mandate to maximize profit rather than primarily promote social responsibility.

The decision whether to employ a person or an AI, even where the two are capable of functioning interchangeably, will therefore be a complex one. Nevertheless, these are precisely the sorts of decisions that businesses are skilled at making – estimating uncertain future costs and making decisions as rational economic actors. Tort liability will only be one factor to consider when businesses are deciding whether to automate. But, in the aggregate, tort liability will influence AI adoption.

As with some of these other factors, the costs of tort liability may not be straightforward. For instance, a business end user might not be directly liable for harms caused by AI. The AI's manufacturer and other members of the supply chain will generally be liable if the harm was caused by a defect in the AI. By contrast, businesses will generally be liable for negligent harms caused by their employees, although they can attempt to limit this liability by, say, relying on independent contractors whose negligent harms businesses will not usually be liable for.

Yet, even in cases where liability rests with a supplier or an independent contractor, such liability should indirectly impact a business. A manufacturer or retailer might pass along its costs in the form of higher prices, or a business might need to pay an independent contractor more than an employee to have the contractor assume risk. The percentage of cost passed on to the business or consumer should depend on the market and price elasticity for that product. Although tort liability can be indirect and complex, and businesses can purchase insurance to manage risk, this does not change the fact that tort liability has a financial cost that influences behavior.

If both human and AI operators cost a business the same amount to employ, the decision of which to utilize should be neutral. However, if a business introduces the variable of tort liability into the decision, assuming that an AI and person are competitive in terms of safety, a human operator would be the preferred hire. Harms caused by a person will be evaluated in negligence while those same harms caused by an AI will be evaluated in strict liability. It is generally easier to establish strict liability than negligence. Strict liability does not require careless manufacturer behavior, only that a defect be present in a product or its marketing. The law favors people over AI, at least with regard to tort liability. This will hold true as long as AI is treated as an "ordinary product" in which strict liability is – and will be – the default rule.

AI-Generated Torts Should Be Negligence-Based

Holding AI-generated torts to a negligence standard would result in an improved outcome: It would accelerate automation where doing so would improve safety. Of course, moving from a strict liability to negligence standard will have some draw-backs. As mentioned earlier, strict liability creates a stronger incentive for manu-facturers to make safer products, and manufacturers are likely better positioned than consumers to ensure against loss. Indeed, this is why courts initially adopted strict product liability. AI-generated torts, however, differ from other product harms in that automation will result in net safety gains once AI becomes safer than people.

To illustrate this, imagine that an AV with current technology is ten times safer than a human driver. In this case, it would be better that one human driver be replaced by an AV than that the same AV become a hundred times safer than a human driver. To see why this is so, assume a closed system with only two vehicles, where the risk of injury for a human driver is one fatality per 100 million miles driven and the risk of injury for an AV (model C-A) is one fatality per one billion miles driven. C-A is ten times safer than a person. Over the course of ten billion miles driven by the person and C-A, there will be an average of 110 fatalities.

Now, imagine that C-A is improved an additional tenfold, such that its risk of causing injury is reduced to one fatality per 10 billion miles (C-A+). Then, over the course of ten billion miles driven by the person and C-A+, there will be a total of 101 fatalities. If, however, instead of focusing efforts on improving C-A, the human driver is simply replaced with another C-A, then over the course of 10 billion miles driven by two C-A model vehicles, there will be a total of twenty fatalities. Once AI becomes safer than people, and particularly once AI becomes substantially safer than people, automating would result in very significant reductions in accident rates. At some point, it will be preferable to increase the adoption of safer technologies at the cost of weakening the incentive to incrementally improve product safety.

A negligence standard would, nevertheless, still influence manufacturers to improve AI safety in order to reduce their liability. If an AI causes an accident a person would have avoided, the AI's behavior would fall below the standard of reasonable care and result in liability. Of course, automating with AI that is less safe than a person is not desired, and this is a reason why jurisdictions prohibit unrestricted use of fully autonomous vehicles. Because AVs cannot currently outperform human drivers in any condition, their use is limited to controlled settings, a preemptive alternative to waiting for them to cause accidents and then arranging for compensation.

However, to the extent that tort liability is relied on to limit the introduction and use of comparatively less safe technologies rather than regulatory prohibitions, holding AI-generated torts to a negligence standard would have the desired effect: AI manufacturers would be financially liable when their AI causes accidents a person would have avoided. This could occur if AI is mistakenly predicted to be safer than it really is at the time of its rollout, or if there are other compelling reasons to automate. For example, it might be that Tesla has reason to believe its self-driving cars are significantly safer than human drivers, but once its cars enter the marketplace, they fail to meet expectations because, say, Tesla's research fails to consider the reactions of drivers to self-driving vehicles in states other than California.

Even an AI that is generally safer than a person will still cause accidents. If it causes an accident a person would have avoided, this will result in liability. An AV might cause an accident on average once every billion miles compared to a person who might cause an accident every hundred million miles, but any particular accident caused by the AV might still fall below the standard of reasonable care. Manufacturers will likely have the best information available to determine whether it would be better to pay to further reduce accident risks (e.g., whether an additional $10,000 per AV is worth a 1 percent reduction in accident risk, or whether to pay claims for additional accidents).

Higher safety levels will not always be preferable as inefficiently high safety levels might result in prohibitively high prices for consumers. To the extent that society is not satisfied with a manufacturer's risk-benefit analysis on optimum safety levels, nontort mechanisms could be brought to bear, such as regulatory mandates for minimum safety standards. Finally, if risk spreading is a concern, even though businesses are better positioned to acquire insurance, consumers also have options to purchase insurance, particularly in the automobile context.

There is further justification for separating out harms caused by ordinary products like *MacPherson*'s Buick and AI tortfeasors like Uber's AV. Society's relationship with technology has changed. Machines are no longer just inert tools directed by individuals. Rather, in at least some instances, AI is taking over activities once performed by people and causing the same sorts of harm these activities generate.

What distinguishes an ordinary product from an AI tortfeasor in this system are the concepts of independence and control. Autonomous AI is given tasks to complete and functionally determine for itself the means of completing those tasks. In some instances, machine learning can generate unpredictable behavior, such that the means are not predictable either by those giving tasks to AI or even by the AI's original programmers.

Nonetheless, the difference between ordinary products and AI tortfeasors should not be based on predictability, only on social and practical outcomes. It makes no difference to a person run over by a self-driving car what type of AI was operating the vehicle. The physical outcome is the same whether an AI acts according to fixed or expert rules created by programmers or more complex machine learning algorithms such as neural networks that generate new and sometimes unforeseen behaviors. Ultimately, tort law should be functional and aspire to lower accident rates.

Identifying AI-Generated Torts

Not all injuries for which a machine or AI is involved would be AI-generated torts. To illustrate, consider two hypothetical accidents:

(1) A crane operator drops a steel frame on a passerby after incorrectly identifying the location for drop-off.

(2) A crane operator is appropriately manipulating a crane under normal conditions when it tips over and lands on a passerby.

In the first example, as between the machine and the operator, it seems obvious (and it can be assumed) that the operator is at fault (although a creative plaintiff's attorney may argue the crane was negligently designed to allow such an outcome). The machine did not interrupt a direct and foreseeable chain of events set in motion by the operator's action, even though the accident could not have occurred without the machine's involvement, making it a factual cause of the injury in torts vernacular. It was essentially functioning as an extension of the operator. In the second hypothetical, allocating fault is once again intuitively obvious. The machine was at fault rather than the operator. The operator acted with reasonable care, and the injury was due to (again it can be assumed) a flawed crane.

These two scenarios would result in different liability outcomes. In the first, the operator, and possibly the operator's employer, would be liable to the passerby in negligence because the operator failed to exercise reasonable care. In the second, the manufacturer and retailer of the crane would be strictly liable to the passerby, even if the manufacturer had exercised the utmost care in the design and construction of the crane. In both scenarios, an operator was using a crane in much the same way cranes have been used in construction for thousands of years. Granted, today's cranes utilize more sophisticated designs, are built from sturdier materials, and have electric power; nevertheless, the basic dynamic between man and machine has changed little. The cranes used to build skyscrapers, the pulleys used to build the Giza pyramids, and the cranes used to build the Parthenon all involved human operators controlling the movements of a simple or complex machine to redirect and amplify force.

Now imagine a third scenario:

(3) An AI-operated, unmanned crane drops a steel frame on a passerby after incorrectly identifying the location for drop-off.

The law now treats Examples 2 and 3 the same way because they both involve defective products. Yet, in important respects, Examples 1 and 3 are more closely related. They involve the same sort of action and physical result. In Example 2, the machine is being used as a tool. In Example 3, an AI replaces a person, and it performs in essentially the same manner as a person. If the AI were a person, it would be liable in negligence and held to the standard of a reasonable person. Changing how these accidents are treated and holding suppliers of AI tortfeasors to a negligence standard require rules for distinguishing between AI-generated torts and other harms. The goal is to distinguish between cases in which a machine is used as a mere instrument and a person is at fault (Example 1), cases in which an ordinary product is at fault (Example 2), and cases in which there is an "AI tortfeasor" (Example 3).

AI-generated torts could be those cases in which an AI engages in activity that a person could engage in and that acts in a manner that would be negligent for a human tortfeasor. If this rule is applied to the crane examples, Example 1 would result in human liability because the human operator acted carelessly and because the crane did not interrupt a foreseeable chain of events. There would be strict manufacturer liability in Example 2 because a person could not reasonably be substituted for a crane. Example 3 would require negligent manufacturer liability since the AI was automating a task that a person could have performed.

Sometimes this rule will have clear application. For example, an AI that mistakenly "reads" a chest X-ray in place of a radiologist would be occupying the position of a human tortfeasor whereas a malfunctioning X-ray machine would be an ordinary product. In other instances, this distinction would not be clear cut. Electrocardiogram (ECG) machines, a vital feature of emergency rooms where they are used to evaluate patients for heart conditions, often provide interpretation of raw data but generally state that any analysis is preliminary and that health care providers are ultimately responsible for diagnosis.

In the context of the self-driving car, under the most widely adopted framework, vehicles are categorized on a zero to five scale based on "who does what, when."[10] At level zero, the human driver does everything; at level five, the vehicle can perform all driving tasks under all conditions that a human driver can perform. In between, there are various degrees of assistance, control, and interaction between man and machine. So, autonomy exists on a continuum, and while it might be clear in some cases that an AI is acting like a person or an ordinary product, in other cases there might be an overlap of responsibility and decision-making between people and AI.

When an individual and an AI contribute to a harm, they might both be liable, either jointly or individually, in proportion to their wrongdoing. When a human driver and an AI driver are both at fault, as may have been the case when Uber's system failed to stop in time for a pedestrian and the backup driver was watching a TV show, they could be found equally negligent. The sort of analysis that commonly used ECGs perform has value, but it is widely understood not to be at the level of a human physician and is legitimately not intended to replace a human diagnosis. ECGs are better considered an ordinary product and holding them to the standard of a physician would result in their routinely being found liable for medical negligence. This would likely result in manufacturers' no longer providing analysis that now has value to doctors.

However, a supplier should not be able to avoid liability simply by disclaiming liability for a product that is obviously automating human activity. Also, it should not be necessary for an AI to actually replace a human operator for negligence to apply, but it should be sufficient that an AI is performing a task that a person could reasonably do. Thus, if a new taxi company goes into business using only a fleet of AVs, the company would not have replaced human operators with AI; AI would be doing work that human drivers could have done. By contrast, the portions of the taxis other than the self-driving software (e.g., the engine) could not be reasonably substituted for a person. So, while the software operating the self-driving taxi could qualify as an AI tortfeasor, the other parts of the vehicle could not.

The negligence test should focus on whether the AI's act was negligent rather than whether the AI was negligently designed or marketed. Again, the AI is taking the place of a person in the traditional negligence paradigm, and this would treat the AI more like a person than a product. It makes no difference to an accident victim what an AI was "thinking," only how it acted. Accident victims have a right to demand careful conduct, regardless of how well an AI tortfeasor might have been designed.

There is another important reason why focusing on an AI's act is more appropriate than focusing on its design: As discussed in Chapter 1, many AI systems, such as those utilizing machine learning, are becoming increasingly complex and have limited explainability, making it difficult or impractical for anyone, including an AV supplier, to determine why a self-driving car, say, ran a red light. But if the harmful act stems from defective software, then such a determination might be necessary to prove a product has a defect and thus to establish liability. Even worse, it will almost certainly be substantially more challenging for a plaintiff to establish a product defect than it would be for a defendant. The plaintiff might need to hire (quite expensive) experts to investigate a self-driving car's AI, which presupposes a court would permit external access to a supplier's (likely) proprietary AI system. The cost of such an inquiry probably puts it beyond the feasibility of accidents without at least hundreds of thousands or millions of dollars in damages.

In the US system (although not the UK system), plaintiffs usually cannot recover their legal costs even when they prevail in court. For some injured victims then, lawyer and expert fees would exceed any likely recovery, which means that some meritorious claims would not be pursued. By contrast, a negligence test focused on an AI's act and whether it falls below the standard of a reasonable person would simply ask if the AV ran a red light and whether a reasonable person would have done the same. This is a far simpler and less expensive case to prove.

Of course, it is sometimes possible when alleging negligence, or even a defective product, for a plaintiff to prove her case with inference on the basis of reason, logic, bad behavior by a party, or common sense. As one example, a legal doctrine known as *res ipsa loquitur* – "the thing speaks for itself" – allows circumstantial evidence to permit an inference that a defendant is at fault. For example, if a barrel falls off a building striking a pedestrian and causing harm, the pedestrian may have a difficult or impossible time proving what caused the accident. But, because barrels tend not to fall off buildings absent careless behavior, the mere fact of the barrel's falling may be sufficient to establish negligence absent compelling contradictory evidence from a defendant.

Similarly, when a medical instrument is left in a patient after surgery, it tends to be adequate to establish negligence, even though a patient may have no way of proving what occurred. However, inference, including through application of *res ipsa loquitur*, is not a panacea to the challenges posed by AI tortfeasors – at least as currently applied by courts. For example, *res ipsa loquitur* is not recognized by every state. Some states require that a defendant have exclusive control over a product (which can be problematic with the involvement of multiple parties), and not all states allow for the presumption of a product defect. There are similar restrictions on the use of inference more generally in many jurisdictions to avoid speculation and unfairness to defendants. Just because an accident occurs with a product does not necessarily mean there was a defect.

Financial Liability

AI cannot be directly financially liable for its harms whether in strict liability or negligence since it does not have property rights. In fact, AI is owned as property and would not be influenced by the specter of liability in the way a person can be influenced. For the purposes of financial liability, the AI's manufacturer and other members of the supply chain should still be responsible for satisfying judgments under standard principles of product liability law, which already has rules for allocating liability in complex cases where several parties contribute to the design and production of an ordinary product, or where several parties are involved in the distribution chain. Those rules could apply in a case where Apple and Delphi jointly design self-driving car software, which General Motors licenses and incorporates in its vehicles, and an independent retailer leases the vehicles to Lyft. Default liability rules could be altered by businesses in the supply chain through contracts. This would be particularly likely to occur in cases where manufacturers and retailers are large, sophisticated entities, such that General Motors could indemnify Apple, Delphi, and Lyft in return for more favorable licensing and leasing terms.

Alternately, the AI's owner could be liable for its harms, which would be somewhat akin to treating AI tortfeasors as employees and making owners liable under theories of vicarious liability – that is, when someone is held responsible for the actions of another person. It is particularly easy to imagine owners' purchasing insurance for harms caused by AI in the context of a self-driving car. Insurance policies may soon come with a rider (or discount) for AV software. Owner liability may further incentivize the production of autonomous AI given that manufacturers would have less liability, but this could also reduce adoption since owners would be taking on that liability. These two effects may offset each other if reduced manufacturer liability were to result in lower purchase prices. Ultimately, owner liability is not an ideal solution because owners may be the most likely victims of AI tortfeasors, and because manufacturers are still in the best position to improve product safety and weigh the risks and benefits of new technologies.

In practice, the economic impact of different liability standards for accidents by self-driving cars will be seen in insurance costs. Insurers base their premiums on risk, and insurance rates will decrease for self-driving cars, perhaps even increase for human drivers, once self-driving cars become significantly safer than human drivers. This should have a nudging effect on the adoption of self-driving cars, as financially sensitive individuals consider automobile premiums in deciding whether to drive. Even lower premiums for self-driving cars would be expected to the extent that they are judged under a more lenient negligence standard, thus further incentivizing their adoption. If manufacturers and retailers rather than car owners are held responsible for accidents, the burden of insurance would shift from owners to manufacturers, although this cost may then be reflected in higher car purchase prices.

Alternatives to Negligence

The shift from a strict liability to negligence standard is not the only means of encouraging automation. The government could provide financial incentives to manufacturers and retailers to promote the creation and sale of safer technologies, since in other contexts, such efforts have been effective at promoting innovation. For example, incentives could take the form of grants for research and development, loans to build production facilities, enhanced intellectual property rights, prizes, preferential tax treatments, or government guarantees.

The government could even provide credits to consumers for purchasing self-driving cars, similar to what it did under the Car Allowance Rebate System (CARS), better known as "cash for clunkers," which provided consumers' trading in old vehicles with vouchers between $3,500 and $4,500 to purchase new cars. It was a $3 billion US federal program designed as a short-term economic stimulus to benefit US automobile manufacturers and to promote safer, cleaner, more fuel-efficient vehicles. Ultimately, while critics dispute the effectiveness of the program at stimulating the economy and promoting domestically produced automobiles, CARS did succeed at improving fuel-efficiency and safety, and it was popular with consumers. In a similar manner, the government could provide consumers who trade in their conventional vehicles with vouchers to purchase self-driving cars.

Even if incentives are limited to tort liability, there are still alternatives to shifting to negligence. Manufactures could have their liability limited through state or federal tort reform acts that would place caps on damages, limit contingency fees (the ability of lawyers to obtain a percentage of a client's recovery as a fee for services), mandate periodic payments, or reduce the statute of limitations (the time limit for suing). Mandatory regulations are another mechanism by which the government can promote safety. This could involve requirements that industries achieve minimum safety targets or adopt certain technologies. For example, human driving could be prohibited when self-driving cars become ten or a hundred times safer than human drivers. Regulatory solutions may be most appropriate when the benefits of automation are overwhelming, and when it is undisputed that automation would result in massive safety gains.

Yet, there is reason to think that shifting from strict liability to negligence without mandating automation is a preferred mechanism. It is both a consumer- and business-friendly solution. While consumers may have more difficulty seeking to recover for accidents, they should also benefit from a reduced risk of accidents. Most consumers would probably prefer to avoid harm rather than improve their odds of receiving compensation. Businesses would have lower costs associated with liability (which could also result in lower consumer prices).

A market shift to negligence would not require government funding, additional regulatory burdens on industry, or new administrative responsibilities. It would provide an incremental solution that relies on existing mechanisms for distributing liability and builds upon the established common law. There may be less risk that shifting from strict liability to negligence would produce unexpected outcomes than with more radical regulatory solutions. Therefore, a negligence standard for AI should be a politically feasible solution. Ultimately, to the extent that policymakers agree that automation should be promoted when it improves safety, there is no need to rely on a single mechanism. Such a shift could operate alongside government grants for research and development and consumer credits and combined with direct regulations in certain instances.

3 REASONABLE ROBOTS

If, for instance, a man is born hasty and awkward, is always having accidents and hurting himself or his neighbors, no doubt his congenital defects will be allowed for in the courts of Heaven, but his slips are no less troublesome to his neighbors than if they sprang from guilty neglect.

– Oliver Wendell Holmes Jr.

When Negligence Is Strict

Negligence may function almost like strict liability for people with below-average abilities. Individuals with special challenges and disabilities may not be capable of always exercising ordinary prudence and may be unable to maintain "a certain average of conduct." This issue was at the heart of a case in 1837, *Vaughan v. Menlove*, that concerned a defendant who lacked average intelligence. The defense argued that it would be unfair to hold him to the standard of an ordinary person, and that he should instead be held to the standard of a person with low intelligence. The court disagreed, holding that ordinary prudence should apply in every case of negligence. As famed judge Oliver Wendell Holmes Jr. later articulated, "The law considers ... what would be blameworthy in the average man, the man of ordinary intelligence and prudence, and determines liability by that. If we fall below the level in those gifts, it is our misfortune."[11] This remains the case today: A modern defendant cannot generally escape liability for causing a motor vehicle accident because she has slow reflexes, poor vision, or anxiety while driving.

There are benefits to such a rule. Logistically, as the court noted in *Vaughan*, it is difficult to take individual peculiarities into account when determining a defendant's actual mental state. Better for administrative purposes to work with an external, objective standard than to prove individual capacities and state of mind. Substantively, the rule reinforces social norms, creates greater deterrent pressure, and strengthens each person's right to demand normal conduct of others. As Holmes expressed, damages caused by individuals with reduced capabilities are no less burdensome than those caused by ordinary people. This rule thus benefits the general welfare but at the cost of telling some individuals that their best is not good enough. Those with diminished capabilities drive at their own peril, or they "should perhaps refrain from driving at all."[12]

The New Hasty and Awkward

Collectively, people are not the best drivers, even when they do not drink behind the wheel, fall asleep on the highway, or collide into police cars while playing Pokémon GO. But compared to AI? It will not be long before AI is safer than the average driver, and then safer than any human driver. Principles of harm avoidance suggest that once it becomes practical to automate, and that doing so is safer, an AI should become the new "reasonable person" or standard of care. In practice, this would mean that the defendant would be judged against what an AI would have done instead of judging his action against what a reasonable person would have done. For instance, today a defendant may not be liable for striking a child running in front of her car if a reasonable driver would not have been able to stop. But that person would soon be liable under the exact same circumstances if an AV would have, more likely than not, prevented the injury. In fact, it may be that the AV is only able to prevent such an accident because it has superhuman abilities, such as software capable of ultrafast decision-making and access to external cameras that expand peripheral view beyond that of a person.

With the reasonable person test, jurors are asked to put themselves in the place of a reasonable person and decide what that person would have done. It may be a challenge for a juror to follow that reasoning in the case of a reasonable robot, but it is a far less nebulous and fictional concept than the reasonable person. The term "reasonable" in the context of an AI is an anthropomorphism to assist people conceptually. To take a simple case, imagine an individual driving on dry pavement at forty miles per hour and then colliding with a child who runs into the road 150 feet ahead of the driver's vehicle. To determine whether the driver is liable under the reasonable robot standard, a plaintiff could present a jury with evidence that the same make and model of car that is being operated by automated software under the same conditions stops in about 100 feet. This means that the reasonable robot would not have collided with the child, and the human driver would be liable. Juries would not need to take distraction into account, the reaction time of AI would be known, and the breaking distance could be standardized if the driver's vehicle could not directly be compared because it was not a vehicle type operated by self-driving software.

A defendant may argue that it is unfair for his best efforts to result in liability. A reasonable robot standard essentially makes people strictly liable for their accidental harms. This is the case now for below-average drivers, and the underlying rationale for the rule will not change when an above-average human driver becomes a below-average driver due to AI. It may appear unfair to impose liability on human drivers for doing their best, but it would be more unfair to prevent accident victims from recovering for harms that would have been avoided had a robot been driving. It does not matter to an accident victim whether he was run over by a person or an AI.

Tort liability would not prohibit people from driving even when AVs become substantially safer than people. If that were a desired outcome, it could be accomplished through a legislative ban on human driving. Instead, an AI standard of care would mean that people drive at their own risk, and this would have a significant impact on behavior. If a driver causes an accident, he will be liable for the resultant damages. A tort-based incentive may be preferable to an inflexible statutory mandate because there are benefits to human driving unrelated to accidents, such as for promoting freedom and autonomy. Individuals who particularly value their freedom may still choose to drive and accept the consequences of their accidents. Making individuals and businesses effectively strictly liable for their harms will discourage rather than outright prevent certain undertakings. In the context of the self-driving car, it would likely result in fewer human drivers as insurance rates for traditional vehicles would become more expensive relative to self-driving cars.

A rule requiring automation at the time it first becomes available would be too harsh. AI may be prohibitively expensive or only available in limited quantities, which is likely early in a technology's lifecycle. It would be unfair to penalize people for not automating when doing so would be impossible or impractical. Therefore, to introduce a reasonable robot standard, a plaintiff should have to show that a person was performing a task that could be performed by an AI and that it would have been practicable for the defendant to automate. This means that a defendant would not be judged against the standard of an AI if (1) no such AI existed at the time of the accident, (2) no AI was available to the defendant, (3) an AI was prohibitively expensive, or (4) there were other overriding interests for not automating (e.g., regulatory requirements for a human driver). If Tesla could manufacturer a completely safe AV at a cost of $1 million, it would not be reasonable to require that all consumers automate.

Reasonable People Use AI

An alternative to the reasonable robot standard could be the reasonable person using an AI. For example, once self-driving cars become safer than people, a jury may find that it is unreasonable to drive yourself rather than to use an AV. When the reasonable person using an AI standard is applied to the earlier hypothetical involving a child who runs into the street, the human driver's negligence would not be based on failing to stop in 100 feet as a self-driving car would have; rather, liability would be based on his driving in the first place. A reasonable person would not have driven; a reasonable person would have chosen to automate.

Under either the reasonable person or reasonable robot standard, a human driver would be compared with a self-driving car but in different ways. With the reasonable robot standard, courts would evaluate the human driver's proximally harmful act, whereas they would evaluate the human driver's initial decision to automate based on the reasonable person standard (a bad decision would then be considered the harmful act). Maintaining the reasonable person standard would be more in line with the existing negligence regime. Yet, while it would be conceptually easier to keep the reasonable person standard, in practice it would be less desirable. The goal is to compare the harmful act of the person and AI, not target the initial decision to automate. It is problematic to base liability on the decision to automate because it must focus on the question of whether automation is either generally or situationally beneficial. A general focus fails to consider instances where a person will outperform an AI, and a situational focus must still compare the harmful act of a person versus an AI.

AI is and will be safer at automating not all but certain activities. For instance, an AI that is working to diagnose disease may be superior to physicians at detecting some conditions but not others. Self-driving cars may be safer than human drivers on average but not safer than professional or above-average drivers. AVs may also be safer under most conditions but may be relatively poor at, for example, driving off-road. So, while automation may generally improve safety, optimal accident reduction may require a mix of AI and human activity. Suppose, for example, an AV is ten times safer than a human driver generally but only half as safe as a human driver in icy conditions. Now, imagine a human driver encounters a patch of black ice and causes an accident under circumstances when she would not be negligent by comparison to a reasonable human driver. If courts were to hold her to the standard of a reasonable robot, she would escape liability if the AI would have been unable to avoid the accident (which is likely if the AI is half as safe in icy conditions). If the reasonable person using an AI test focuses on whether an AI is generally safer, however, she would be liable. This test would conclude that it would have been unreasonable not to use a self-driving car since it is generally safer. This would penalize human action even when it would be preferred.

Alternately, the reasonable person using an AI evaluation could be situational. For instance, it could be reasonable not to use an AI but only in icy conditions. However, this is just a more convoluted version of the reasonable robot test, because it requires evaluating whether an AI would be safer than a person in a particular instance. This essentially asks how the AI would have acted in a situation – which would be the application of the reasonable robot standard. It would then require asking, based on that knowledge (which may be impractical for a person to have), whether an earlier decision to automate was reasonable. In the black ice hypothetical, it could require that the driver know in advance of activating or deactivating self-driving software whether there are icy conditions and how the AI would perform in icy conditions to determine if the risk of using the AI in icy conditions outweighs the benefits of using it for other parts of the trip.

The Reasonable Robot Standard for AI Tortfeasors

AI tortfeasors should be held to a negligence standard, and their acts ought to be compared to those of a reasonable person. Further, the reasonable person standard should be replaced with the reasonable robot standard once automation is practicable and AI is safer than the average person. Eventually, this means that AI tortfeasors will be held to the reasonable robot standard. For instance, if a self-driving Audi collides with a child who ran in front of the vehicle, the negligence test could take into account the stopping times of self-driving Google cars.

There is more than one way of determining the reasonable robot standard (e.g., considering the industry customary, average, or safest technology). Under any test, this is different than the current strict liability standard where the inquiry focuses on whether a product is defectively designed or its properties falsely represented. As AI improves, the reasonable robot standard will grow stricter, which is alright, because once AI is exponentially safer than a person, it is likely that AI tortfeasors will rarely cause accidents. While the economic impact of tort liability on automation adoption may be slight, the primary effect of the reasonable robot standard would be to internalize the cost of accidents on human tortfeasors.

Nonetheless, there may be instances in which it will still make sense to apply the reasonable person standard to AI tortfeasors. As described earlier, there will be cases in which a human defendant would not be judged against the standard of an AI, such as where automation is prohibitively expensive or AI is not widely available. In these cases, it would not be appropriate to hold an AI tortfeasor to a higher standard than a human defendant. In some industries and for certain types of automation, it may take decades – a lifetime, even – after the introduction of autonomous technologies for their use to become routine.

Further Thoughts

Applying a principle of AI legal neutrality to tort law, as seen with tax law, will guide AI's development and adoption and help ensure its social utility, but careful consideration needs to be given to its application. In tort law, the challenges are not the same as with tax law, and the two bodies of law have different underlying concerns, goals, and solutions. The primary policy goal with tort law is to structure liability in order to optimize accident deterrence.

In the future, there are likely to be few activities for which AI cannot outperform people. Self-driving cars will eventually be a thousand times safer than the best human driver, at which point AI will cause so little harm that the economics of negligence versus strict liability will be irrelevant to AI manufacturers. AI will have become so ubiquitous that the constantly improving reasonable robot should set the benchmark for most or all areas of accident law, thereby preventing countless losses and injuries. It has become acceptable for more than a million people a year to die in traffic accidents worldwide, but only because a reasonable alternative has not yet been within reach. But there could soon be a world where practically no one dies from unintended injury, the third-leading cause of death. We would then just be left to deal with the leading two causes of death: cardiovascular disease and cancer. Artificial inventors, a different type of AI, may eliminate those as well.

4

Artificial Inventors

Computers are useless. They can only give you answers.
— Pablo Picasso

In 2019, a team of patent attorneys, in a legal test case spearheaded by this book's author, announced they had filed the first patent applications in several jurisdictions worldwide that explicitly claimed inventions generated by an AI (the Artificial Inventor Project).[1] The applications listed the AI's owner as the patent applicant (and therefore the owner of any future patents) and the AI as the inventor. As of the time of writing, these applications are still pending (or appealing initial rejections). Already, "inventive AI" generates patentable inventions under circumstances in which the AI, rather than a person, meets the requirements to qualify as an inventor, but it remains unclear whether an "AI-generated invention" can be patented. In the United States, there is no statute addressing AI-generated invention, no case law directly on the subject, and no relevant policy by the responsible administrative agency, the US Patent and Trademark Office (Patent Office). Nor, in 2019, did there appear to be a statute specifically about AI-generated invention anywhere else in the world. However, almost every country in the world requires that a patent application list a natural person as an inventor, a requirement designed to ensure the right of human inventors to be acknowledged.

Historically, academics have argued against allowing protections for AI-generated inventions on the grounds that machines do not respond to incentives and that AI inventorship could chill human invention. Some patent offices have also criticized the very idea of AI-generated inventions. In 2019, a spokesperson for the European Patent Office stated,

> It is a global consensus that an inventor can only be a person who makes a contribution to the invention's conception in the form of devising an idea or a plan in the mind . . . . The current state of technological development suggests that, for the foreseeable future, AI is . . . a tool used by a human inventor . . . . Any

change ... [would] have implications reaching far beyond patent law, i.e., to authors' rights under copyright laws, civil liability and data protection.[2]

The principle of AI legal neutrality suggests that the law should allow intellectual property protections for AI-generated inventions. Although the prospect of a patent would not directly motivate AI to invent, it will inspire the people who build, own, and use AI. Intellectual property protections for AI output will incentivize the development of inventive AI that will lead to innovations and scientific advances – the primary purpose of the patent system. This is particularly critical for the day when AI will be a meaningful source, or even the primary means, of generating new inventions. In addition, an AI should be listed as an inventor when it otherwise meets inventorship criteria to maintain the integrity of the patent system and to protect the rights of human inventors. Although a person's taking credit for an AI's work would not be unfair to the AI, it would be unfair to human inventors because it would dilute the nature of inventorship and equate the work of legitimate human inventors with people's asking AI to solve a problem. Finally, the default owner of any patents on an AI's invention should be its owner.

This chapter, divided into three sections, begins by examining instances in which AI has created patentable inventions. The second section reviews the case law related to nonhuman authorship of copyrightable material in the absence of laws on AI inventorship. It argues for intellectual property protections for AI-generated inventions and further contends that an AI should qualify as a legal inventor. Section 3 addresses some implications of AI inventorship: coexistence and competition of human and AI inventors, redefinition of human inventive activity, and industry consolidation of intellectual property.

1 AI-GENERATED INVENTIONS

Early Examples

In 1994, computer scientist Stephen Thaler disclosed an AI architecture he called a "Creativity Machine," a computational paradigm that he argued "came the closest yet to emulating the fundamental mechanisms responsible for idea formation."[3] A Creativity Machine combines an artificial neural network that generates novel output in response to self-stimulation of the network's connections with a "critic" network that monitors the first network's output. The critic network can evaluate this output for novelty compared to the AI's existing knowledge base and provide feedback to the first network to continue or stop developing some novel output. This results in an AI that "brainstorms" new and creative ideas after it alters (perturbs) the connections within its neural network. An example of this phenomenon occurred after Thaler exposed a Creativity Machine to his favorite music, and the AI produced eleven thousand new songs in a single weekend.

Thaler compared a Creativity Machine and its processes to a human brain and consciousness. The two artificial neural networks mimic the human brain's major cognitive circuit: the thalamo-cortical loop. In a simplified model of the human brain, the cortex generates a stream of output (or consciousness) and the thalamus brings attention (or awareness) to ideas of interest. Like the brain, a Creativity Machine is capable of generating original patterns of information rather than simply associating patterns and of adapting to new scenarios without additional human input. The AI's software is, to a degree, self-assembling. Thaler argued his AI is very different from a program that simply generates a spectrum of possible solutions to a problem combined with an algorithm to filter for the best ideas generated, though such a program would be another method for having an AI develop novel ideas.

The Creativity Machine paradigm was the subject of Thaler's first patent. The second patent filed in his name was titled "Neural Network Based Prototyping System and Method."[4] Thaler is listed as the patent's inventor, but he stated that a Creativity Machine generated the patent's invention (Creativity Machine's Patent). The Creativity Machine's Patent application was first filed on January 26, 1996, and granted on December 22, 1998. As one of Thaler's associates observes in response to the Creativity Machine's Patent, "Patent Number Two was invented by Patent Number One. Think about that. Patent Number Two was invented by Patent Number One!"[5]

Creativity Machines are credited with numerous other inventions in addition to the Creativity Machine's Patent: the cross-bristle design of the Oral-B CrossAction toothbrush, new physical materials, and devices that search the Internet for messages from terrorists. The Creativity Machine's Patent is interesting because if Thaler's claims are accurate, then the Patent Office has already granted a patent for an invention created by a nonhuman inventor – and as early as 1998. Also, the Patent Office had no idea it did so. On the advice of his attorneys, Thaler listed himself as the inventor on the patent and did not disclose the Creativity Machine's involvement at the time of filing.

Thaler's Creativity Machine has not been the only early example of AI-generated invention. Software modeled after the process of biological evolution, known as genetic programming, has also succeeded in independently generating patentable results. Evolution is a creative process that relies on a few simple processes: mutation, sexual recombination, and natural selection. Genetic programming emulates these same methods digitally to achieve machine intelligence. It delivers human-competitive intelligence with a minimum amount of human involvement. As early as 1996, genetic programming succeeded in independently generating results that were the subject of past patents. By 2010, there were at least thirty-one instances in which genetic programming generated a result that duplicated a previously patented invention, infringed a previously issued patent, or created a patentable invention. In seven of those instances, genetic programming infringed or duplicated the functionality of a twenty-first-century invention, some of which were on the cutting edge of research in their respective fields.

The Patent Office granted a patent for another AI-generated invention on January 25, 2005.[6] The invention was created by the "Invention Machine" – the moniker for a genetic programming–based AI developed by John Koza, a computer scientist and pioneer in the field of genetic programming as well as the inventor of the scratch-off lottery ticket. A 2006 article in *Popular Science* about Koza and the Invention Machine notes that the AI "has even earned a U.S. patent for developing a system to make factories more efficient, one of the first intellectual property protections ever granted to a nonhuman designer."[7] The Invention Machine generated the content of the patent and an improved controller (a common component of electrical products) design without human intervention and in a single pass.[8] It did so without a database of expert knowledge and without any knowledge about existing controllers. It simply required information about basic components (such as resistors and diodes) and specifications for a desired result (performance measures such as voltage and frequency). With this information, the Invention Machine proceeded to produce different outputs that were measured for fitness (whether an output met performance measures).

Once again, the Patent Office had no idea of the AI's role in the Invention Machine's patent. Koza did not disclose the Invention Machine's involvement. Like Stephen Thaler, Koza has stated that his legal counsel advised him at the time that his team should consider themselves inventors, despite the fact that "the whole invention was created by a computer."[9] In fact, Koza has claimed the Invention Machine created several patentable inventions.[10]

The Creativity Machine and the Invention Machine are early examples of AI inventors, but patents may have been granted on even earlier AI-generated inventions. An article published in 1983 describes experiments with an AI program known as Eurisko, in which the program "invent[ed] new kinds of three-dimensional microelectronic devices ... novel designs and design rules have emerged."[11] Eurisko was an early expert AI system for autonomously discovering new information. Programmed to operate according to a series of rules known as heuristics, Eurisko was able to discover new ones, which it used to modify its own programming. Programmers provided Eurisko with knowledge of basic microchips and simple rules and evaluation criteria. The AI then combined existing chip structures together to create several novel designs, which were then evaluated for interest and either retained or discarded. Stanford University filed a patent for one of Eurisko's chip designs in 1980 but abandoned the filing for unknown reasons in 1984.[12] As with other reported instances of patent applications for AI-generated inventions, the patent application was filed on behalf of natural persons. In this case, the individuals who built a physical chip based on Eurisko's design.

In another example, a 1989 PhD dissertation disclosed a

systematic computational approach to innovative design of engineered artifacts in general ... comparable to human inventions ... a computer program called TED ... [which] is the inventor of its systems in the sense that it generates the structure (topology) of the system 'from scratch.' The synthesis process is modeled as a heuristic search conducted in a state-space of all possible design versions (design states). TED explores one design possibility after another in a systematic fashion, looking for a solution to the design requirements.[13]

Alexander Kott, TED's developer, noted that TED rediscovered at least two significant and well-known inventions and also generated previously unknown and nontrivial designs.

Modern Examples

The preceding examples are decades old. Subsequent improvements in AI should have led to a significant increase in the number of AI-generated inventions. Consider, for instance, more recent results produced by IBM's AI Watson. Watson was an AI developed by IBM to compete on the game show *Jeopardy!* In 2011, ancient history in AI terms, Watson beat former *Jeopardy!* winners Ken Jennings and Brad Rutter on the show, earning a million dollars in the process. Since then, the "Watson" brand has evolved to incorporate a variety of AI systems and technologies, although it is sometimes marketed by IBM as if it were a single AI. For simplicity, it will be treated as a single AI system here.

Watson was initially largely structured as an "expert system," one way of designing symbolic AI that solves problems in a specific domain using logical rules derived from the knowledge of experts. These were a major focus of AI research in the 1980s. The expert system–based chess-playing programs HiTech and Deep Thought defeated chess masters in 1989, paving the way for another famous IBM AI, Deep Blue, to defeat world chess champion Garry Kasparov in 1997. But Deep Blue had limited utility. It was solely designed to play chess. The machine was permanently retired after defeating Kasparov.

IBM now describes Watson as one of a new generation of machines capable of "computational creativity"[14] that can generate "ideas the world has never imagined before."[15] Watson "generates millions of ideas out of the quintillions of possibilities, and then predicts which ones are [best], applying big data in new ways."[16] This is a fundamentally different type of AI than the Creativity Machine or the Invention Machine. Watson utilizes a more conventional architecture of logical deduction combined with access to massive databases containing accumulated human knowledge and expertise. Although Watson is not modeled after the human brain or evolutionary processes, it might also be capable of generating inventions.

By 2014, Watson was being applied to more pragmatic challenges, such as running a food truck. IBM developed new algorithms for Watson and incorporated a database with information about nutrition, flavor compounds, molecular structures of foods, and tens of thousands of existing recipes. This design permits Watson to generate recipes in response to users' inputting a few parameters such as ingredients, dish (e.g., burgers or burritos), and style (e.g., British or dairy-free). On the basis of this user input, Watson proceeds to generate a staggeringly large number of potential food combinations. It then evaluates these preliminary results based on novelty and predicts quality to generate a final output. Some of Watson's discoveries in food science may be patentable. Patents are granted for any "new and useful process, machine, manufacture, or composition of matter, or any new and useful improvement thereof."[7] Food recipes could qualify as patentable on this basis because lists of ingredients combine to form new compositions of matter or manufacture, and the steps involved in creating food could be considered a process.

To be patentable, however, an invention must not only contain patentable subject matter but also be novel, nonobvious, and useful. This is challenging to achieve in the case of food recipes since there is a finite number of ingredients and people have been putting ingredients together for a very long time. To be granted a patent for one of its recipes, Watson would have to create a recipe that no one had previously created and that was not an obvious variation on an existing recipe. Still, people do obtain patents on food recipes. The fact that some of Watson's results have been surprising to its developers and human chefs is encouraging in this regard because unexpected results are one of the factors considered in determining whether an invention is nonobvious.

Watson is not, however, limited to competing on *Jeopardy!* or developing food recipes. IBM reports it has made Watson broadly available to software application providers, enabling them to create services with Watson's capabilities. Watson now, among other tasks, assists with financial planning, helps clinicians develop treatment plans for cancer patients, conducts research in drug discovery, and acts as a personal travel concierge. Specifically, in drug discovery, Watson has identified novel drug targets and new indications for existing drugs. In doing so, Watson might be generating patentable inventions either autonomously or collaboratively with human researchers, and it is not the only AI system involved in modern innovation.

In 2019, researchers at Flinders University in Australia reported that they had used AI to develop a flu vaccine approved for human trials.[8] The research team created an AI, Sam, to recognize effective and ineffective flu vaccines. They then created a second AI to develop trillions of potential vaccine candidates, which Sam narrowed to the ten most promising candidates. The human team synthesized and tested these candidates over the course of a few weeks rather than directly screening millions of compounds. The AI reportedly identified a more effective vaccine, sped up the discovery process, and substantially reduced costs.

Companies like BenevolentAI now report similarly applying AI to the entire drug discovery process.

Where Is the Law?

There have been credible claims of AI-generated invention for decades, and AI has improved exponentially in that time. Therefore, it would seem as if there should be a number of lawsuits involving AI-generated inventions and a well-developed legal framework for them. This is not the case. The Artificial Inventor Project involves the first and still only applications disclosing AI-generated inventions. What this suggests is that applicants are choosing not to disclose the role of AI in the inventive process. The choice to do this is most likely due to legal uncertainty: Inventions without a natural person as an inventor could be ineligible for patent protection and enter the public domain after disclosure. In other words, existing laws, or the lack of them, have likely driven activity underground.

An AI user who wishes to obtain a patent on an AI-generated invention may choose to identify herself as an inventor to protect it and her. Indeed, as Stephen Thaler and John Koza reported, some of the earliest applicants for patents on AI-generated inventions were advised to list themselves as inventors, despite their own admissions that they themselves did not meet inventorship criteria. Patent offices are supposed to accept reported inventors at face value in the ordinary course of things, unless challenged by third parties. Where an AI has autonomously created something, it is unlikely to complain about not being listed as an inventor. AI's role in an invention would probably only become an issue if a patent is disputed in court.

2 INTELLECTUAL PROPERTY RIGHTS FOR AI-GENERATED INVENTIONS

Inventorship Requirements and the Inventive Process

All patent applications require one or more named inventors who must be "individuals"; an artificial person such as a corporation cannot be an inventor. Inventors own their patents as a form of personal property, which they may transfer by assignment of their rights to another entity. A patent grants its owner "the right to exclude others from making, using, offering for sale, or selling the invention throughout the United States or importing the invention into the United States."[19]

For a person to be an inventor in the United States, the person must contribute to an invention's conception, which refers to "the formation in the mind of the inventor of a definite and permanent idea of the complete and operative invention as it is thereafter to be applied in practice."[20] It is "the complete performance of the mental part of the inventive act."[21] After conception, someone with ordinary skill in the invention's subject matter (e.g., a chemist if the invention is a new chemical compound) should be able to reduce the invention to practice. That is, he should be able to make and use the invention from a description without extensive experimentation or additional inventive skill. Individuals who simply reduce an invention to practice by, for example, describing an already conceived invention in writing or building a working model from a description do not qualify as inventors.

Although AI is commonly involved in the inventive process, in most cases AI essentially works as a sophisticated, or not-so-sophisticated, tool such as when it functions as a calculator. In those instances, AI can assist a human inventor to reduce an invention to practice but cannot participate in the invention's conception. Even when it plays a more substantive role in the inventive process by analyzing data in an automated fashion, retrieving stored knowledge, or recognizing patterns of information, AI may still fail to contribute to the conception of an invention. Like a person, an AI's involvement in the inventive process could be conceptualized on a spectrum. At one end, AI is a tool assisting an inventor; on the other, it functionally automates conception.

Consider a hypothetical inspired by the Watson "insights" business model. Clients give their data to IBM, IBM runs the data through Watson, and Watson generates insights that might be patentable and belong by contract to the client. In this sort of scenario, it may not always be clear who the inventor of an insight is – or that anyone qualifies as an inventor. The client is probably not an inventor as simply commissioning research and handing over data do not generally qualify for inventorship. Perhaps, an inventor is the person who programmed Watson, but probably not if he were developing a program with general problem-solving capabilities and without his specifically addressing the problem it would be applied to and the eventual solution.

Deeming a programmer as an inventor is even more difficult in cases where a group of people spread over time and space contributes to developing an AI. Perhaps, the person who is "using" Watson is an inventor but not if he is just asking a computer to solve a known problem. Finally, the person who recognizes the significance of an insight might be an inventor, particularly if he must use skill to select one of many AI outputs, but this does not seem appropriate where the importance of output is obvious and requires no further human effort.

In this scenario, at least some of the time, an otherwise patentable invention is created under circumstances such that no natural person traditionally qualifies as an inventor. IBM has not reported that Watson has generated any AI-generated inventions, but another Fortune 100 company, Siemens, has. The company notes that it has been unable to file for protection on AI-generated inventions because it cannot identify a natural person who qualifies as an inventor on those inventions.[22]

Legal Barriers to AI Inventorship

The US Congress is empowered to grant patents on the basis of the Patent and Copyright Clause of the Constitution, which enables Congress "[t]o promote the Progress of Science and useful Arts, by securing for limited Times to Authors and

Inventors the exclusive Right to their respective Writings and Discoveries."[23] The clause also provides an explicit rationale for granting patent and copyright protections, namely to encourage innovation under an incentive theory. The theory goes that people will be more inclined to invent things (i.e., promote the progress of science) if they can receive government-sanctioned monopolies (i.e., patents) to exploit commercial embodiments of their inventions. Having the exclusive right to sell an invention can be, sometimes, quite lucrative.

The Patent Act, which here simply refers to US patent law as a whole, provides at least a couple of challenges to AI's qualifying as an inventor. First, as mentioned earlier in this section, the Patent Act requires that inventors be "individuals." This language has been in place since at least the 1952 legislation that established the basic structure of modern patent law. Legislators at the time were not thinking about AI-generated inventions. The "individual" requirement assists with determining ownership and ensures that inventors, who are commonly under assignment obligations to their employers, are listed on patents. Being acknowledged as an inventor can have significant meaning as a moral right and economic value as a signal of productivity.

Second, patent law jurisprudence requires that inventions be the result of a "mental act," a feat for AI that is questionable. In a nutshell, it remains unclear whether an AI that is autonomously conceiving of a patentable invention could legally be an inventor. The situation may play out differently in jurisdictions that do not require an inventor to be a natural person like Monaco and Cypress, which are both member states of the European Patent Office.[24]

Nonhuman Authors of Copyrightable Material

The Patent Act does not directly address the issue of an AI-generated invention. The Patent Office has never issued guidance addressing the subject, and there is no case law on the issue of whether an AI could be an inventor. There is, however, guidance available from the related issue of nonhuman authorship of copyrightable works. Since at least 1973, the US Copyright Office has formally conditioned copyright registration on human authorship,[25] although applicants report that the Copyright Office has rejected submissions for AI-generated works as far back as 1957.[26]

In its 2014 compendium, the Copyright Office published an updated "Human Authorship Requirement," which states the following:

> To qualify as a work of "authorship" a work must be created by a human being. . . .
> The Office will not register works produced by nature, animals, or plants. . . .
> Similarly, the Office will not register works produced by a machine or mere mechanical process that operates randomly or automatically without any creative input or intervention from a human author.[27]

The requirement is based on jurisprudence that dates long before the invention of modern computers to the *In re Trade-Mark* cases in 1879, in which the US Supreme

Court interprets the Patent and Copyright Clause to exclude the power to regulate trademarks. In interpreting this clause, the court states that the term "writings" may be construed liberally but notes that only writings that are "original, and are founded in the creative powers of the mind[,]" may be protected.[28]

The issue of nonhuman authorship was implicit in the case of *Burrow-Giles Lithographic Co.* v. *Sarony* in 1884. In that case, a defendant company accused of copyright infringement argued that a famous photograph of Oscar Wilde did not qualify as a "writing" or as the work of an "author." The company further argued that even if a visual work could be copyrighted, a photograph should not qualify for protection because it was just a mechanical reproduction of a natural phenomenon and thus could not embody the intellectual conception of its author. The court ultimately disagreed, noting that all forms of writing "by which the ideas in the mind of the author are given visible expression" are eligible for copyright protection.[29] The court further stated that although ordinary photographs may not embody an author's "idea," in this particular instance, the photographer had exercised enough control over the subject matter that it qualified as an original work of art. Therefore, the case explicitly addresses whether the camera's involvement negated human authorship, and it implicitly deals with the question of whether a camera can be considered an author. Though it seems unwise to put much emphasis on nonbinding judicial statements from the Gilded Age to resolve the question of whether nonhumans can be authors, the Copyright Office still cites *Burrow-Giles* in support of its Human Authorship Requirement.

The Copyright Office first publicly addressed the issue of AI authors in 1966 when the Register of Copyrights, Abraham Kaminstein, questioned whether AI-generated works should be copyrightable. Kaminstein reported that, by 1965, the Copyright Office had received applications for AI-generated works including an abstract draw-ing, a musical composition, and compilations that were, at least partly, the work of computers. Kaminstein did not announce a policy for dealing with such applications but suggested the relevant issue should be whether an AI was merely an assisting instrument (as with the camera in *Burrow-Giles*) or whether an AI conceived and executed the traditional elements of authorship.

In 1974, Congress created the Commission on New Technological Uses of Copyrighted Works (CONTU) to study issues related to copyright and AI-generated works. At that time, copyright law did not even address the issue of whether computer software should be copyrightable – a far more urgent and financially important problem. With regard to AI authorship, CONTU wrote in 1979 that there is no need for special treatment of AI-generated works because AI is not autonomously generating creative results without human intervention; AI simply functions as a tool to assist human authors.

CONTU also declared that autonomously creative AI was not immediately foreseeable and concluded that "works created by the use of computers should be afforded copyright protection if they are original works of authorship within the Act of 1976."[30] According to the commission, "The author is [the] one who employs the computer."[31] Former CONTU Commissioner Arthur Miller explains that "CONTU did not attempt to determine whether a computer work generated with little or no human involvement is copyrightable."[32]

Congress subsequently codified CONTU's recommendations. Nearly a decade later, in 1986, advances in AI prompted Congress's Office of Technology Assessment (OTA) to issue a report arguing that CONTU's approach was too simplistic and that computer programs are more than "inert tools of creation." The OTA report contended that, in many cases, computers are at least "co-creators." The OTA did not dispute that AI-generated works should be copyrightable, but it did foresee problems with determining authorship.

To date, there have yet to be any US cases specifically about whether copyright can subsist in an AI-generated work, but one case sought to challenge the Copyright Office's Human Authorship Requirement. The *Monkey Selfies* are a series of images that a Celebes crested macaque named Naruto took of itself in 2011 using equipment belonging to the nature photographer David Slater. Slater made conflicting reports about the circumstances under which the photographs were taken, but he eventually claimed that he staged the photographs by setting up a camera on a tripod and leaving a remote trigger for the macaque to use. He subsequently licensed the photographs, claiming he owned their copyright. Other parties then reposted the photographs without his permission and over his objections, asserting that Slater could not copyright the images without having taken them directly. On December 22, 2014, public discourse over these events prompted the Copyright Office to specifically list the example of a photograph taken by a monkey as something not protectable under its revised and renamed Human Authorship Requirement.

In September 2015, People for the Ethical Treatment of Animals (PETA) filed a copyright infringement suit against Slater on behalf of Naruto asserting that it was entitled to copyright ownership of the *Monkey Selfies*. On January 28, 2016, US District Judge William Orrick dismissed PETA's lawsuit against Slater on the grounds that Naruto lacked standing to sue. He also deferred to the Copyright Office's interpretation that the macaque was not an "author." Judge Orrick considered PETA's arguments to the contrary but ruled that animal authorship is "an issue for Congress and the President."[33] PETA appealed this decision, but the appellate court also dismissed the case on the basis that Naruto did not have standing to sue. The court held that animals only have standing to sue if an act of Congress plainly states they can sue, which is not the case with the Copyright Act. In so ruling, the court avoided weighing-in on the substantive merits of nonhuman authorship.

AI-Generated Works in the United Kingdom

While the US Copyright Office declines to provide copyright protection for AI-generated works, the United Kingdom passed a law in 1988 that took the opposite approach. UK Copyright Law makes a special provision for AI-generated works, defined as those "generated by a computer in circumstances such that there is no human author of the work[s]," [34] and provides that "in the case of a literary, dramatic, musical or artistic work which is computer-generated, the author shall be taken to be the person by whom the arrangement necessary for the creation of the work are undertaken." [35]

Two cases in the United Kingdom considered AI-generated works under the law in place before 1988. In 1985's *Express Newspapers plc* v. *Liverpool Daily Post & Echo*, the *Daily Express* newspaper had distributed cards with a five-letter code that recipients could check against a daily AI-generated newspaper grid to see if they had won a prize. The defendant newspaper was sued for copyright infringement after copying these grids, and it argued in defense that because they were AI-generated grids that they could not be protected by copyright. The judge in the case, Justice John Whitford, rejected that argument, stating that "The computer was no more than the tool by which the varying grids of five-letter sequences were produced to the instructions, via the computer programs, of [the programmer]. It is as unrealistic [to suggest the programmer was not the author] as it would be to suggest that, if you write your work with a pen, it is the pen which is the author of the work rather than the person who drives the pen." [36] He further noted "that a great deal of skill and indeed, a good deal of labour went into the production of the grid and the two separate sequences of five letters." [37]

Interestingly, Justice Whitford had chaired a report in 1977 that argues that the proper approach to AI-generated works is to "look on the computer as a mere tool in much the same way as a slide rule or even, in a simple sense, a paint brush. A very sophisticated tool it may be, with considerable powers to extend man's capabilities to create new works, but a tool nevertheless." [38] The report further contends that the AI programmer and the person who provided the data to the AI should be the authors of any resultant works.

Only one case since the enactment of the UK's current copyright law in 1988 has considered authorship of AI-generated works. In 2006's *Nova Productions Ltd* v. *Mazooma Games Ltd*, the parties were competing manufacturers of pool video games. [39] The plaintiff claimed copyright in the graphics of the game and the frames that were generated by AI based on player commands. The judge in this case, Justice David Kitchin, considered the frames to be computer-generated works even though a person designed the components. He held the author of the works was the company director responsible for designing the game, rather than the player who "contributed no skill or labour of an artistic kind." [40] Even here, limited consideration was given to the protection of AI-generated works because the defendant was not contesting the existence or ownership of copyright in the frames.

Giving AI the Go to Incentivize Innovation

Treating AI-generated inventions as patentable and recognizing AI as an inventor would be consistent with the constitutional rationale for patent protection by encouraging innovation under an incentive theory. Patents on AI-generated inventions will have substantial value independent of the value of AI itself, and this will motivate businesses and computer scientists to develop and use inventive AI. In turn, it will generate more innovation for society. By contrast, without protection for AI-generated inventions, companies' needing a patent might be unable to use (or unwilling to risk using) inventive AI in research and development even if it outperforms human researchers. Patent law seeks to incentivize invention, and the most valuable invention of all time to incentivize might be inventive AI in the form of artificial general intelligence and superintelligence. A hundred years, according to pessimists (or longer), is too long to wait for an AI that might go on to provide the cure for all human disease and the solution to climate change.

An up-front innovation incentive is not the only benefit to patents. Permitting patents on AI-generated inventions will promote disclosure of information and commercialization of new products. If AI owners do not have the legal ability to obtain patent protection, they might choose to protect inventions as trade secrets without any public disclosure. Likewise, businesses might not pursue developing inventions into commercial products without patent protection. In the pharmaceutical and biotechnology industries, for example, most expenses in commercializing a new product are incurred during the clinical testing process required to obtain regulatory approval for marketing – that is, after the product is invented.

Finally, permitting AI inventors will protect the integrity of the patent system and the moral rights of human inventors. Intellectual property protection is also justified, or criticized, on the basis of moral or noneconomic rights, particularly in jurisdictions other than the United States. Moral rights protect interests ranging from owning the fruit of one's labor under Lockean theories to protecting an author's or inventor's personality on the basis of theories advanced by philosophers such as Emmanuel Kant and Georg Hegel, which say that individuals express their "wills" and develop through their interactions with external objects. Someone could develop as a person through the process of writing a book and come to see the book as an extension of herself, and if someone were to take credit for the book, or if the book were altered to support violent and extremist political beliefs, this could cause her injury. In this example, the law would have failed to protect the author's moral rights, and the theories for such an approach support the use of intellectual property rights to prevent authors and inventors from having their ideas misappropriated or altered in objectionable ways.

In the case of AI-generated inventions, people appear to be taking credit for the work of machines. This encourages dishonestly among applicants and allows people to receive underserved credit. While it is not unfair to an AI, it may be unfair to other people, particularly when AI-generated inventions become commonplace. If being a patent inventor comes to mean little more than putting a name on something generated by Watson, then individuals who are inventing without AI will not have their accomplishments appropriately recognized. Further, if the law acknowledges an AI as an inventor, it will simultaneously credit the developers of that AI and recognize them for the achievements of their creations. Compare this to how parents' or teachers' take pride in their children's or students' success without taking direct credit for their future works.

Costs of AI-Generated Inventions

Arguments in support of patentability for AI-generated invention are based mainly on the dominant narrative justifying the grant of intellectual property protection. This account, however, has been criticized, particularly by academics. Patents can result in significant social costs through the establishment of monopolies. Whether the benefit of patents as an innovation incentive outweighs its anticompetitive costs, or whether patents have a net positive effect on innovation, likely varies between industries, areas of scientific research, and inventive entities.

Commentators such as Judge Richard Posner have argued that patents are not needed to incentivize research and development in the software industry. Software innovation is often relatively inexpensive, incremental, quickly superseded, produced without patent incentives, protected by other forms of intellectual property, and associated with a significant first mover advantage (the initial product on the market captures users and people are reluctant to later switch platforms). Likewise, patents may be unnecessary to spur innovation in university settings where inventors are motivated to publish their results for prestige and the prospect of academic advancement. Similarly, AI-generated inventions can develop due to nonpatent incentives. AI developers have all sorts of noneconomic motivations to create inventive AI: to enhance their reputations, satisfy scientific curiosity, or collaborate with peers. Businesses might realize significant value from AI-generated inventions, even in the absence of patent protection.

Of course, patents on AI-generated inventions will not be dispositive to every act of innovation; they may further encourage activities that would have otherwise occurred on a smaller scale over a longer timeframe. Even though individuals and businesses do not always behave as rational economic actors, in the aggregate it is likely that providing additional financial incentives to spur the development of inventive AI will produce a net benefit. This, at least, is the justification for why the law grants patents to people. The arguments in support of human-generated patents apply with equal force to AI-generated patents.

It Does Not Matter Whether AI Thinks

Judicial doctrine says that invention involves a mental act, but this should not prevent patents on AI-generated inventions or AI inventorship. The precise nature of a "mental act requirement" is unclear. Courts have discussed mental activity largely from the standpoint of determining when an invention is made, not whether it is inventive. They have not been using terms precisely or meaningfully in the context of AI-generated inventions. Would a mental act requirement necessitate that AI engage in a process that results in inventive output – which it does – or would AI somehow need to mimic human thought? If the latter, it is unclear what the purpose of such a requirement would be except to exclude nonhumans (for which a convoluted test is unnecessary).

Stephen Thaler argues that a Creativity Machine closely imitates the architecture of the human brain. Should that mean that a Creativity Machine's inventions should receive patents while Watson's do not? Or, if a Creativity Machine does not meet the threshold for engaging in mental activity, would a computer scientist have to design a completely digitized version of the human brain (which may not be the most effective way to structure an inventive AI)? There is a slippery slope in determining what constitutes a thinking AI, even without considering deficits in our understanding of human cognition.

The problem of speaking precisely about thought with regard to computers was identified by Alan Turing, who in 1950 considered the question, "Can machines think?" He found the question to be ambiguous and the term "think" to be unscientific in its colloquial usage. Turing decided the better question to address is whether an individual can tell the difference between responses from a computer and an individual; rather than asking whether machines think, he asked whether machines can perform in the same manner as thinking entities (i.e., people). Turing referred to his test as the "Imitation Game," though it has also come to be known as the Turing test.

Although the Turing test has been the subject of criticism, Turing's analysis from more than sixty years ago demonstrates that a mental act requirement would be ambiguous, challenging to administer, and of uncertain utility. Incidentally, the Patent Office administers a sort of Turing test, which inventive AI has successfully passed. The Patent Office receives descriptions of inventions and then judges whether they are nonobvious – a measure of creativity and ingenuity. In the case of the Invention Machine's patent, it was already noted that "January 25, 2005[,] looms large in the history of computer science as the day that genetic programming passed its first real Turing test: The examiner had no idea that he was looking at the intellectual property of a computer."[41]

The most important reason a mental act requirement should not prevent AI-generated invention and AI inventorship is that the patent system should be indifferent to the means by which invention comes about. Congress concluded this in 1952 when it abolished the Flash of Genius doctrine, which had been used by the federal courts as a test for patentability for more than a decade. It held that in order to be patentable, a new device, "however useful it may be, must reveal the flash of creative genius, not merely the skill of the calling."[42] The doctrine was interpreted to mean that an invention must come into the mind of an inventor in a "flash of genius" rather than as a "result of long toil and experimentation."[43] As a commentator at the time noted,

The standard of patentable invention represented by [the Flash of Genius doctrine] is apparently based upon the nature of the mental processes of the patentee-inventor by which he achieved the advancement in the art claimed in his patent, rather than solely upon the objective nature of the advancement itself.[44]

The Flash of Genius test was an unhelpful doctrine because it was vague and difficult for lower courts to interpret, involved judges' making subjective decisions about a patentee's state of mind, and made it substantially more difficult to obtain a patent. The test was part of general hostility toward patents exhibited by mid-twentieth-century courts, which caused Supreme Court Justice Robert Jackson to note in a dissent that "the only patent that is valid is one which this Court has not been able to get its hands on."[45]

Criticism of this state of affairs led President Franklin D. Roosevelt to establish a National Patent Planning Commission to study the patent system and make recommendations for its improvement. In 1943, the commission reported with regard to the Flash of Genius doctrine that "patentability shall be determined objectively by the nature of the contribution to the advancement of the art, and not subjectively by the nature of the process by which the invention may have been accomplished."[46] The Patent Act of 1952, by adopting this recommendation, legislatively disavowed the Flash of Genius test. In the same manner, patentability of AI-generated inventions should be based on the inventiveness of an AI's output rather than on a clumsy anthropomorphism because patent law should be interested, like Turing, in a functionalist solution.

Incidentally, even a requirement for biological intelligence may be a poor way to distinguish between AI and human inventors. Functioning biological computers do not yet exist, but all the necessary building blocks have been created. In 2013, a team of Stanford University engineers created a biological version of an electrical transistor. Mechanical computers use numerous silicon transistors to control the flow of electrons along a circuit to create binary code. The Stanford group created a biological version with the same functionality by using enzymes to control the flow of RNA proteins along a strand of DNA. Envisioning a future in which AI can be entirely biological, there seems to be no principled reason why a biological – but not a mechanical – version of Watson should qualify as an inventor.

A Dynamic Interpretation of Current Law

If AI-generated inventions should be patentable and AI should be an inventor, then these outcomes ought to be permitted under a dynamic interpretation of the law. Such an approach would be consistent with the Founders' intent in enacting the Patent and Copyright Clause, and it would interpret the Patent Act to further that purpose. In addition, this interpretation would not run afoul of the chief objection to a dynamic statutory interpretation, namely that it interferes with reliance and predictability and the ability of citizens "to be able to read the statute books and know their rights and duties."[47] Permitting AI inventors would allow additional patent applications rather than retroactively invalidate previously granted patents, and there is naturally less reliance and predictability in patent law than in many other fields given that it is a highly dynamic subject area that struggles to adapt to constantly changing technologies.

This would not be the first time that patent law has been the subject of a dynamic interpretation. For example, in the landmark 1980 case of *Diamond* v. *Chakrabarty*, the Supreme Court was charged with deciding whether genetically modified organisms could be patented. It held that a categorical rule's denying patent protection for "inventions in areas not contemplated by Congress ... would frustrate the purposes of the patent law."[48] The court noted that Congress chose expansive language to protect a broad range of patentable subject matter.

Under that reasoning, AI inventorship and AI-generated inventions should not be prohibited based on statutory text designed to protect the rights of human inventors. It would be particularly unwise to prohibit AI inventors on the basis of literal interpretations of texts written when AI-generated inventions were unforeseeable. If AI inventorship and AI-generated inventions are to be prohibited, it should only be on the basis of sound public policy. Drawing an analogy from the copyright context, just as the terms "writings" and "authors" have been construed flexibly in interpreting the Patent and Copyright Clause, so too should the term "inventors" be afforded the flexibility needed to effectuate constitutional purposes.

3 IMPLICATIONS OF AI-GENERATED INVENTIONS

Ownership of AI-Generated Inventions

Ownership rights to AI-generated inventions (in the event they are patentable) should vest in an AI's owner because it would be most consistent with the way personal property (including both AI and patents) is treated. If a person owns a machine that produces property, then he would own that property whether it is a loaf of bread or a trade secret (leaving aside more complex cases in which multiple parties are involved or he does not have rights to the machine's input [whether baking soda or another party's data]). This ownership could be taken as a starting point, although parties should be able to contract around this default, and as AI-generated inventions become more common, negotiations over these inventions may become a standard part of contract negotiations. These parties can ultimately work out the most efficient allocation of rights between themselves, so long as property entitlements are clearly allocated. However, a default ownership rule is still necessary to minimize overall transaction costs.

A default ownership rule in favor of an AI's owner may further encourage innovation compared to, say, a user or developer ownership default. For instance, IBM has made Watson available to numerous developers without transferring Watson's ownership. To the extent that Watson creates patentable results as a product of its interactions with users, the promotion of user access should result in more innovation. There is theoretically no limit to the number of users that Watson, as a software program that can be copied, could interact with at once. If Watson invents while under the control of a non-IBM user and the "default rule" assigns the invention to the user, IBM could be encouraged to restrict user access.

In contrast, assigning the invention to IBM would be expected to motivate IBM to further promote access. If IBM and a user were negotiating for a license to Watson, the default rule could result in a user's paying IBM an additional fee for the ability to patent results or receiving a discount by sticking with the default. It could also be that Watson invents jointly along with a user in which case a system of default assignment to an AI's owner could result in both IBM and the user co-owning the resulting patent. Where inventive AI is not owned by large enterprises with sophisticated attorneys, it is more likely the default rule will govern the outcome.

Coexistence and Competition

IBM has bragged to the media that Watson's question-answering skills are good for more than annoying Alex Trebek. The company sees a future in which fields like medical diagnosis, business analytics, and tech support are automated by question-answering software like Watson. Just as factory jobs were eliminated in the 20th century by new assembly-line robots, [Watson's Jeopardy competitors] were the first knowledge-industry workers put out of work by the new generation of "thinking" machines. "Quiz show contestant" may be the first job made redundant by Watson, but I'm sure it won't be the last.[49]

– Ken Jennings

AI's expansion into domains previously occupied only by people threatens to displace human inventors. Consider a hypothetical involving antibody therapy. Antibodies are small proteins the immune system naturally makes, primarily to neutralize pathogens such as bacteria and viruses. They are Y-shaped proteins largely similar to one another in structure, although antibodies contain an extremely variable region that binds to target structures. Differences in that region are the reason different antibodies bind to different targets (e.g., why one antibody binds to a cancer cell while another to a common cold virus). The body generates antibody diversity in part by harnessing the power of random gene recombinations and mutations (much as genetic programming does), and then it selects for antibodies with a desired binding (much as genetic programming does).

After human researchers discovered the antibody structure and the technologies to manufacture antibodies in the 1970s, they began to create antibodies for diagnostic and therapeutic purposes, the latter of which can, among other functions, block cell functions, modulate signal pathways, and target cancer cells. There are now many artificially manufactured antibodies approved to treat a variety of medical conditions. All the major biological (made from a living organism or its products) "blockbuster" drugs, those that earn in excess of a billion dollars a year, are antibodies.

The interesting thing about antibodies from an AI-generated invention perspective is that a finite number of antibodies exist. There are, at least, billions of possible antibodies, enough natural diversity for the immune system to function and keep human researchers active for the foreseeable future. Even so, the body can string together only so many combinations of amino acids (the building blocks of proteins) to generate an antibody. With enough computing power, an AI could sequence every conceivable antibody that could ever be created – even if the number of sequences were in the trillions. The task might be relatively simple for a powerful-enough computer, but it would be impossible for the largest team of human researchers without some AI assistance.

Patents are granted to those inventions that are new, nonobvious, and useful. In a scenario where all these sequences are publicly disclosed, this could be enough to keep anyone from being granted a patent on a "new" antibody because no future sequence could be considered new (assuming the sequence data are considered an anticipatory disclosure). Patents on antibody structure are often the most important protection on a biologic drug. If this disclosure were to occur, an AI would have preempted human invention in an entire scientific field. At the same time, by itself the sequence data would not allow an AI's owner to obtain his own patents. The utility of an invention must be known in addition to the sequence.

Yet, the day when an AI will be able to predict the binding qualities of every conceivable antibody may not be far away. Right now, modern AI systems are able to model and predict antibody binding – that is, the likelihood that a certain antibody will bind to a particular epitope (e.g., a receptor on a cancer cell). If an AI could both sequence every possible antibody and determine how each one could be usefully applied, then it may be enough to obtain patents on each of those antibodies. This could effectively allow an AI owner to patent the cure for cancer. Human cancers may be curable by antibodies so long as they are a match for a particular cancer.

Automation Will Refocus Human Activity

In the hypothetical scenario about antibody therapy, society would gain access to all possible future knowledge about antibody structure at once rather than waiting decades or centuries for individuals to discover these sequences. Early access to antibody sequences could prove a tremendous boon to public health if it leads to the discovery of new drugs. And, it should be noted that some antibody sequences may never be identified without AI. In the short term, AI inventors should refocus rather than inhibit human inventive activity. Scientists who are working on developing new antibody structures may shift to studying how the new antibodies work, or finding new medical applications for those antibodies, or perhaps studying more complex proteins beyond the capability of AI to comprehensively sequence. Unless, and until, AI starts broadly outperforming human researchers, there will be plenty of room for people to invent – all with net gains to innovation.

Antibody therapy is just one example of how AI could preempt invention in a field. A sophisticated-enough AI could do something similar in the field of genetic engineering by creating random sequences of DNA. Living organisms are a great deal more complex than antibodies, but the same fundamental principles apply. A powerful-enough AI could model countless different DNA sequences, inventing new life-forms in the process. In fact, on a smaller scale, this is something genetic programming already does. Although results have been limited by the computationally intense nature of the process, this will change as AI continues to improve (e.g., quantum computers). By creating novel DNA sequences, genetic programming would perform the same function as nondigital genetic programming – natural evolution.

Dealing with Industry Consolidation

Inventive AI may result in greater consolidation of patents in the hands of large corporations. Imagine that IBM's AI Watson can sequence every conceivable antibody, analyze a human cancer, and then successfully match the cancer with an antibody from its library to effectively treat the disease. Essentially, IBM might be able to patent the cure for cancer, receiving a twenty-year monopoly (the term of a patent) in return for publicly disclosing the information a competitor would need to duplicate Watson's invention. Undoubtedly, this would profoundly disrupt the medical industry and could lead to market abuses.

Nevertheless, these are not reasons to disfavor AI-generated invention. The benefit to society is that it would have the cure for a disease that kills more than half a million people in the United States each year. Such a breakthrough might never come about if inventive AI is not able to compete because of concerns over monopolies. These concerns are legitimate, but there are better ways of addressing them such as protections that safeguard consumers against activities like price gouging and supply shortages. One such protection, for example, permits the government to issue compulsory licenses, which grant competitors the right to practice an invention by paying a royalty. Inventive AI activity may increase the need for compulsory licenses. Ultimately, the most important protection may be that, as discussed in the next Chapter, it will become more difficult to receive patents once inventive AI becomes a standard part of research and development.

Further Thoughts

It is important that there be a legal framework that continues to incentivize the generation of intellectual property in a world with inventive AI. The principle of AI legal neutrality suggests that works by AI are no less important to encourage, and that allowing patents on AI-generated inventions will result in broad social gains for people. Moreover, acknowledging AI as an inventor when it functionally invents will maintain the value and meaning of human inventorship. Such a framework will do more than address an academic concern; it will provide certainty to businesses, provide fairness to research, and promote the progress of science. In the words of Thomas Jefferson, "Ingenuity should receive a liberal encouragement."[50] What could be more ingenious than artificial inventors?

5

Everything Is Obvious

Prediction is very difficult, especially about the future.
– Niels Bohr

Chapter 4 focuses on today's AI-generated invention. This chapter considers what happens when tomorrow's inventive AI becomes a standard part of research and development. The impact will be tremendous, not only on innovation but also on patent law. Right now, patentability is determined based on what a hypothetical noninventive skilled person would find obvious. The skilled person, similar to the reasonable person standard in tort law, represents the average worker in the scientific field of an invention. An applicant can only receive a patent if the invention would not be obvious to this skilled person because inventive activity is not supposed to be normal or average. If it were, this would allow patents on inventions that do not require special incentives to create.

However, once the average worker uses inventive AI, or inventive AI replaces the average worker, then the average worker will become inventive. This will create a new challenge because average workers will be capable of routinely generating patentable inventions under today's standard. The principle of AI legal neutrality suggests that the solution is for the skilled person to be an inventive AI once it becomes the standard means of research in a field. This should raise the bar to patentability because inventive AI will more easily find inventions obvious, thus keeping normal activity from being patentable.

Replacing the skilled person standard with AI requires determining what an inventive AI would find "obvious." This exercise may prove difficult to reason through in the same way it is currently done with the standard of an average researcher. A solution would be to change the obviousness inquiry, so that its focus is on economic rather than cognitive factors. An existing vein of critical scholarship has already advocated for such a shift through, for example, greater reliance on real-world evidence of how an invention is received in the marketplace, long-felt but unsolved needs, and the failure of others. To date, an economic standard has not been implemented due to practical challenges, but the widespread use of inventive AI may provide the needed impetus.

Alternately, application of an inventive AI standard could focus on reproducibility. With the skilled person standard, decision makers, in hindsight, need to reason about what another person would have found obvious. This results in inconsistent and unpredictable determinations, similar to the application of Justice Potter Stewart's famously unworkable definition of obscene material – "I know it when I see it." By contrast, whether AI could reproduce the subject matter of a patent application could be far more objective. A more determinate test would allow the Patent Office to apply a single standard consistently and result in fewer judicially invalidated patents.

An inventive AI standard will dynamically raise the current benchmark for patentability in whatever way the test is applied. Inventive AI will be significantly more intelligent than skilled persons and also capable of considering more prior art. An inventive AI standard would not initially prohibit patents, but it would make obtaining them substantially more difficult: A person or an AI would need to have an unusual insight that inventive AI could not easily re-create, developers would need to create increasingly intelligent AI that could outperform standard AI, or most likely invention would be dependent on using specialized, nonpublic sources of data. The patentability bar will continue to rise as AI inevitably improves. If taken to its logical extreme – and given there is no limit to how intelligent AI might become – every invention may one day be obvious to commonly used AI. This would mean no more patents would be issued without some radical change to current patentability criteria.

This chapter has three sections. Section 1 considers the current test for obviousness and its historical evolution. It finds that obviousness is evaluated through the lens of the skilled person, who reflects the characteristics of the average worker in a field. Section 2 considers the use of AI in research and development and proposes a novel framework for conceptualizing the transition from human to AI inventors. Already, inventive AI is competing with human inventors, and human inventors are augmenting their abilities with inventive AI. Section 3 then proposes a framework for implementing the proposed obviousness standard and provides an example of how it would work in practice. It then goes on to consider some of the implications of the new standard. Once the average worker is inventive, there may no longer be a need for patents to function as innovation incentives. To the extent patents accomplish other goals such as promoting commercialization and disclosure of information or validating moral rights, other mechanisms may be found to accomplish these goals with fewer costs.

1 OBVIOUSNESS

Patents are granted for inventions that are new, nonobvious, and useful. Of these three criteria, obviousness is the primary hurdle for most patent applications. Patents are not intended to be granted for incremental inventions, only those that represent a significant advance over existing technology. The reason for this is that patents limit competition and can inhibit future innovation by restricting the use of patented technologies in research and development. To the extent that patents are justified, it is because they are thought to have more benefits than costs. Patents function as innovation incentives, and they can promote the dissemination of information, encourage commercialization of technology, and validate moral rights. Although other patentability criteria contribute to this function, the nonobviousness requirement is the primary test for distinguishing between significant innovations and trivial advances. Of course, it is one thing to express a desire to only protect meaningful scientific advances and another to come up with a workable rule that applies across every area of technology.

Early Attempts

The modern obviousness standard is the culmination of hundreds of years of struggle by the Patent Office, courts, and Congress to separate the wheat from the chaff. As Thomas Jefferson, the first administrator of the patent system and one of its chief architects, wrote, "I know well the difficulty of drawing a line between the things which are worth to the public the embarrassment of an exclusive patent, and those which are not. . . . I saw with what slow progress a system of general rules could be matured."[1] The earliest patent laws focused on novelty and utility, although Jefferson did at one point suggest an "obviousness" requirement. The Patent Act of 1790 was the first patent statute and required patentable inventions be "sufficiently useful and important." Three years later, a more comprehensive patent law was passed – the Patent Act of 1793. The new act did not require an invention be "important" but "new and useful." The 1836 Patent Act reinstated the requirement that an invention be "sufficiently used and important."

In 1851, the Supreme Court adopted the progenitor of the skilled person and the obviousness test – an "invention" standard. *Hotchkiss* v. *Greenwood* concerned a patent for substituting clay or porcelain for a known doorknob material such as metal or wood. The court invalidated the patent, holding that "the improvement is the work of a skillful mechanic, not that of the inventor."[2] The court also articulated a new legal standard for patentability: "Unless more ingenuity and skill . . . were required . . . than were possessed by an ordinary mechanic acquainted with the business, there was an absence of that degree of skill and ingenuity which constitute essential elements of every invention."[3] The court did not, however, give specific guidance on what makes something inventive or the required level of inventiveness.

In subsequent years, the court made several efforts to address these deficiencies with limited success. As the court stated in 1891, "The truth is the word [invention] cannot be defined in such manner as to afford any substantial aid in determining whether any particular device involves an exercise of inventive faculty or not."[4] Or, as one commentator has noted, "It was almost impossible for one to say with any degree of certainty that a particular patent was indeed valid."[5]

Around 1930, the Supreme Court, possibly influenced by a national antimonopoly sentiment, began implementing stricter criteria for determining the level of invention. This culminated in 1941 with the widely disparaged "Flash of Genius" test discussed in Chapter 4 and articulated in *Cuno Engineering* v. *Automatic Devices Corp.*, namely that in order to receive a patent "the new device must reveal the flash of creative genius, not merely the skill of the calling."[6] Extensive criticism of perceived judicial hostility toward patents resulted in President Franklin D. Roosevelt's creating a National Patent Planning Commission to make recommendations for improving the patent system. The Commission's report in 1943 recommended that Congress adopt a more objective and certain standard of obviousness. About a decade later, Congress did.

The Nonobviousness Inquiry

The Patent Act of 1952 established the modern patentability framework. Among other changes to substantive patent law, "The central thrust of the 1952 Act removed 'unmeasurable' inquiries into 'inventiveness' and instead supplied the nonobviousness requirement of Section 103."[7] Section 103 states:

> A patent may not be obtained . . . if the difference between the subject matter sought to be patented and the prior art are such that the subject matter as a whole would have been obvious at the time the invention was made to a person having ordinary skill in the art to which said subject matter pertains. Patentability shall not be negatived by the manner in which the invention was made.[8]

Section 103 legislatively disavowed the Flash of Genius test, codified the sprawling judicial doctrine on "invention" into a single statutory test, and restructured the standard of obviousness in relation to a person having ordinary skill in the art. However, while Section 103 may be more objective and definite than the earlier standard, the meanings of "obvious" and "a person having ordinary skill" were not defined and in practice has proven "often difficult to apply."[9]

The Supreme Court first interpreted the statutory nonobviousness requirement in *Graham* v. *John Deere* (1966) and its companion cases, *Calmar* v. *Cook Chemical* (1965) and *United States* v. *Adams* (1966). The court articulated a framework for evaluating obviousness as a question of law based on the following underlying factual inquiries: (1) the scope and content of the prior art, (2) the level of ordinary skill in the prior art, (3) the differences between the claimed invention and the prior art, and (4) objective evidence of nonobviousness. This framework remains applicable today. Of note, the *Graham* analysis does not explain how to evaluate the ultimate legal question of nonobviousness beyond identifying underlying factual considerations.

In 1984, the newly established US Court of Appeals for the Federal Circuit, the only appellate-level court with jurisdiction to hear patent case appeals, devised the "teaching, suggestion and motivation" (TSM) test for obviousness. Strictly applied, this test only permits an obviousness rejection when prior art explicitly teaches, suggests, or motivates a combination of existing elements into an invention. The TSM test protects against hindsight bias because it requires an objective finding in the prior art. In retrospect, it may be easy for an invention to appear obvious by piecing together bits of prior art using a patent application as a blueprint. In *KSR v. Teleflex* (2006), the Supreme Court upheld the *Graham* analysis but rejected the Federal Circuit's exclusive reliance on the TSM test. The court instead endorsed a flexible approach to obviousness in light of "the diversity of inventive pursuits and of modern technology."[10] Rather than approving a single definitive test, the court identified a nonexhaustive list of rationales to support a finding of obviousness. This remains the approach to obviousness today.

A Person Having Ordinary Skill in the Art

Determining the level of ordinary skill is critical to assessing obviousness. The more sophisticated the skilled person, the more likely an invention is to appear obvious. Thus, it matters a great deal whether the skilled person is a "moron in a hurry" or the combined masters of an invention's scientific field. The skilled person has never been precisely defined, although there is judicial guidance. In *KSR*, the Supreme Court described the skilled person as "a person of ordinary creativity, not an automaton." The Federal Circuit has explained that the skilled person is a hypothetical person presumed to have known the relevant art at the time of the invention. The skilled person is not a judge, amateur, person skilled in remote arts, or a set of "geniuses in the art at hand" but "one who thinks along the line of conventional wisdom in the art and is not one who undertakes to innovate."[11]

The Federal Circuit has provided a list of nonexhaustive factors to consider in determining the level of ordinary skill: (1) "type[s] of problems encountered in the art," (2) "prior art solutions to those problems," (3) "rapidity with which innovations are made," (4) "sophistication of the technology," and (5) "educational level of active workers in the field." In any case, one or more factors may predominate, and not every factor will be relevant. The skilled person standard thus varies according to the invention in question, its field of art, and researchers in the field. In the case of a simple invention in a field where most innovation is created by laypersons, for instance, a device to keep flies away from horses, the skilled person might be someone with little education or practical experience. By contrast, where an invention is in a complex field with highly educated workers such as chemical engineering or pharmaceutical research, the skilled person may be quite sophisticated.

Analogous Prior Art

What constitutes prior art is also central to the obviousness inquiry. On some level, virtually all inventions involve a combination of known elements. The more prior art can be considered, the more likely an invention is to appear obvious. Prior art must fall within the definition for anticipatory references under Section 102 of the Patent Act and must additionally qualify as "analogous art"[12] to be considered for the purposes of obviousness. Section 102 contains the requirement for novelty in an invention and explicitly defines prior art.

An extraordinarily broad amount of information qualifies as prior art, including any printed publication made available to the public prior to filing a patent application. Courts have long held that inventors are charged with constructive knowledge of all prior art. No real inventor could have such knowledge; nevertheless, the social benefits of this rule are thought to outweigh its costs. Granting patents on existing inventions could prevent the public from using something it already had access to and could remove knowledge from the public domain.

For the purposes of obviousness, prior art under Section 102 must also qualify as analogous. In other words, the prior art must be in the field of an applicant's endeavor or reasonably pertinent to the problem with which the applicant was concerned. An inventor would be expected to focus on this type of information. The analogous art rule better reflects practical conditions and ameliorates the harshness of the definition of prior art for novelty, given that prior art references can be combined for purposes of obviousness but not novelty. Consequently, for the purposes of obviousness, the skilled person is presumed to have knowledge of all prior art within the field of an invention as well as prior art reasonably pertinent to the problem the invention solves. Restricting the universe of prior art to analogous art lowers the bar to patentability.

The analogous art requirement is most famously conceptualized in the case of *In re Winslow*, in which the court explained that a decision maker is to "picture the inventor as working in his shop with the prior art references, which he is presumed to know, hanging on the walls around him."[13] Or, as Judge Learned Hand remarked, "the inventor must accept the position of a mythically omniscient worker in his chosen field. As the arts proliferate with prodigious fecundity, his lot is an increasingly hard one."[14]

2 AI IN THE FUTURE OF INVENTION

Timeline to the Inventive Singularity

Until relatively recently, all invention was created by people. If a company wanted to solve an industrial problem, it asked a research scientist, or a team of research scientists, to solve the problem. This is no longer the only option. We are witnessing a transition from human to AI inventors. The following five-phase framework illustrates this transition and divides the history and future of inventive AI into several stages.

Evolution of AI-Generated Invention			
Phase	Inventors	Skilled Standard	Time Frame
I	Human	Person	Past
II	Human > SAI	Augmented Person	Present
III	Human ~ SAI	Augmented Person ~ SAI	Short Term
IV	SAI ~ AGI > Human	Augmented AGI	Medium Term
V	ASI	ASI	Long Term

SAI = Specific Artificial Intelligence; AGI = Artificial General Intelligence; ASI = Artificial Superintelligence; ~ = competing; > = outcompeting

Phase I ended when the first patent was granted for an invention created by an inventive AI, suspected to be around 1998 for an invention autonomously developed by a Creativity Machine. Since there is no obligation to report the role of AI in patent applications, it may never be possible to determine precisely when the first patent was issued for an AI-generated invention. At present, situated in Phase II, AI and people are competing and cooperating at inventive activity. However, in all technological fields, human researchers are the norm and thus best represent the skilled person standard. This phase will reward early adopters of inventive AI in cases where it can outperform human inventors at solving specific problems.

In the meantime, human inventors are widely augmented by AI. A person might design a new engine using AI to perform calculations, search for information, or run simulations on new designs. In these scenarios, the AI does not meet inventorship criteria but does expand the capabilities of a researcher in the same way that human assistants can help reduce an invention to practice. In fact, researchers may rarely be unaided by AI, depending on the industry they work in and the problems they are trying to solve. The more sophisticated the AI, the more it is able to augment the worker's skills. AI may be a particular benefit in areas where discoveries may require the use of tremendous amounts of data or deviate from conventional design wisdom. Along these lines, the company Iprova uses AI, which provides researchers with prior art they would not otherwise consider, to augment them to invent "more diversely."

Phase III, in the near future, will involve increased competition and cooperation between people and AI. Inventive AI will become the norm in some industries and for certain types of problems. For example, in the pharmaceutical industry, Watson now identifies novel drug targets and new indications for existing drugs. Soon, it could be the case that inventive AI is the primary means by which new uses for existing medications are researched. This is a predictable outcome, given the advantage AI has over people at recognizing patterns in very large datasets. However, in this phase, people may still perform the majority of research related to new drug targets. The variation within a broad field like drug discovery can be addressed by defining fields and problems narrowly according to the subclasses currently used by the Patent Office.

Perhaps, twenty-five years from now – based on expert opinion – the introduction of artificial general intelligence (AGI) will usher in Phase IV. As discussed in Chapter 1, existing narrow or specific AI systems focus on discrete problems or work in particular domains. By contrast, AGI would be able to successfully perform any intellectual task a person could. AGI will compete with human inventors in every field, which makes AGI a natural substitute for the skilled person. Even with this new standard, human inventors could continue to invent – just not as much. An inventor might be a creative genius whose abilities exceed the human average or a person of ordinary intelligence who has a groundbreaking insight.

In the event that specific AI outperforms AGI in certain circumstances, specific AI could continue to represent the level of ordinary skill in fields in which specific AI is the standard while AGI could replace the skilled person in all other fields. For example, the screening of a million compounds for pesticide function could lend itself to a brute-force computational approach. Moreover, the two systems will likely be compatible. A general AI system's wanting to play Go could incorporate AlphaGo into its own programming, design its own algorithm like AlphaGo, or even instruct a second AI operating AlphaGo.

AGI will change the human-AI dynamic in another way. If AI is genuinely capable of performing any intellectual task a person could, AI would be capable of setting goals collaboratively with a person, or even by itself. For instance, a person could ask an AI to develop a new pesticide rather than give it specific instructions or provide it with particular data. For that matter, an agrochemical company like Bayer could instruct DeepMind's AI to develop any new technology for its business, or just improve its profitability. Such AI should be able to solve not only problems we know the answers to but also those we do not – perhaps even the ones we do not know exist.

Most importantly, AGI could be set to the task of reprogramming and improving itself. This "recursive self-improvement" should eventually result in artificial super-intelligence, an AI that would far surpass human intelligence in virtually all domains. Ultimately, Phase V will mean the end of obviousness when AGI will have succeeded in developing artificial superintelligence. In this phase, everything will be obvious to a sufficiently intelligent AI, and artificial superintelligence will be able to invent or discover just about anything.

Skilled People Use AI

The skilled person test is in need of an update, given that AI is routinely augmenting the capabilities of human workers. Recall that the factor test for the skilled person includes (1) "type[s] of problems encountered in the art," (2) "prior art solutions to those problems," (3) "rapidity with which innovations are made," (4) "sophistication of the technology," and (5) "educational level of active workers in the field." This test should be amended to include (6) "technologies used by active workers." This would explicitly require decision makers to take into account the fact that human researchers may be augmented with AI in a way that is not currently captured by the test, in essence making them more sophisticated.

The changing use of AI also suggests a change to the scope of prior art. The analogous art test was implemented because it is unrealistic to expect inventors to be familiar with anything more than the prior art in their field as well as the prior art relevant to the problem they are trying to solve.[15] However, an AI is capable of accessing a virtually unlimited amount of prior art. Advances in medicine, physics, or even culinary science could be relevant to solving a problem in electrical engineering. AI augmentation suggests that the analogous art test should be modified, or abolished, once inventive AI is common, and that there should be no difference in prior art for purposes of novelty and obviousness. The scope of analogous prior art has consistently expanded in patent law jurisprudence, and this would complete that expansion.

Once the use of inventive AI that automates research rather than augments researchers is standard, instead of a skilled person's being replaced by an inventive AI, the skilled person standard could incorporate the fact that "technologies used by active workers" include inventive AI. It would be less of a conceptual change to characterize the skilled person as an average worker using inventive AI rather than replacing the skilled person with inventive AI. Under either standard, the result will be the same: The average worker will be capable of inventive activity. Nevertheless, replacing the skilled person with the inventive AI would be preferable because it would emphasize that AI is engaging in inventive activity, not the human worker.

Inventive and Skilled AI

For purposes of patent law, an inventive AI should be one that generates patentable output while meeting traditional inventorship criteria. Under the present framework, inventive AI would not be the equivalent of skilled AI, just as human inventors are not skilled persons. In fact, it should not be possible to extrapolate about the characteristics of a skilled entity from information about inventive AI. Granted, the Federal Circuit once included the "educational level of the inventor" in its early factor-based test for the skilled person, but only until it occurred to the Federal Circuit that "courts never have judged patentability by what the real inventor/applicant/patentee could or would do. Real inventors, as a class, vary in the capacities from ignorant geniuses to Nobel laureates; the courts have always applied a standard based on an imaginary work of their own devising whom they have equated with the inventor."[16]

What then conceptually is a skilled AI? An AI that anthropomorphizes to the various descriptions that courts have given for the skilled person? Such a test could focus on the way an AI is designed or how it functions. For instance, a skilled AI could be a Good Old-Fashioned AI as opposed to an AI like DeepMind's that functions unpredictably. However, basing a rule on how an AI functions may not work for the same reason the Flash of Genius test failed. Even leaving aside the significant logistical problem of attempting to figure out how an AI is structured or how it generates particular output, patent law should be concerned with whether an AI is generating inventive output, not what is going on inside the AI. If a symbolic and a connectionist AI were both able to generate the same inventive output, there would be no reason to favor one over the other.

Alternately, the test could focus on an AI's capacity for creativity. For example, Microsoft Excel plays a role in a significant amount of inventive activity, but it is not innovative. It applies a known body of knowledge to solve problems with known solutions in a predictable fashion (e.g., multiplying values together). However, while Excel may sometimes solve problems that a person could not easily solve without the use of technology, it lacks the ability to perform even at the level of an average worker. Excel is not the equivalent of a skilled AI – it is an automaton incapable of ordinary creativity.

Watson in clinical practice may be a better analogy for a skilled worker. Watson is analyzing a patient's genome and providing treatment recommendations. The problem Watson is solving may be more complex than multiplying a series of numbers, but it has a known solution. Watson is identifying known genetic mutations from a patient's genome and then suggesting known treatments based on existing medical literature. Watson is not innovating because it is being applied to solve problems with known solutions, adhering to conventional wisdom. Yet, other Watson activity might be inventive: for instance, giving it unpublished clinical data on patent genetics and actual drug responses and then tasking it with determining whether a drug works for a genetic mutation in a way that has not yet been recognized. Traditionally, such discoveries have been patentable. Watson may be situationally inventive depending on the problem it is solving.

It may be difficult to identify an actual AI that has a "skilled" level of creativity. To the extent an AI is creative, in the right circumstances any degree of creativity could result in inventive output. To be sure, this is similar to the skilled person. A person of ordinary skill, or almost anyone, may have an inventive insight. Characteristics can be imputed to a skilled person, but it is not possible the way the test is applied to identify an actual skilled person or to definitively say what she would have found obvious. The skilled person test is simply a theoretical device for a decision maker.

Assuming a useful characterization of a skilled AI, to determine that a skilled AI represents the average worker in a field, decision makers would need information about the extent to which such an AI is used. Obtaining this information may not be practical. Patent applicants could be asked generally about the use and prevalence of

AI in their fields, but it would be unreasonable to expect applicants to already have, or to obtain, accurate information about general industry conditions. The Patent Office, or another government agency, could attempt to proactively research the use of AI in different fields, but this may be costly. The Patent Office lacks expertise is this activity, and its findings would inevitably lag rapidly changing conditions. Ultimately, there may not be a reliable, low-cost source of information about skilled AI.

Inventive Is the New Skilled

Having inventive AI replace the skilled person may better correspond with real-world conditions. There are inherent limits to the number and capabilities of human workers, but inventive AI is likely to be a software program, which may not cost much – if anything – to copy. Once IBM sees that Watson outperforms the average industry researcher, IBM may simply copy Watson. Copies of Watson could replace individual workers, or a single Watson could do the work of a large team of researchers, replacing an existing workforce. Indeed, as mentioned earlier in a noninventive setting, IBM reports that Watson can interpret a patient's entire genome and prepare a clinically actionable report in ten minutes compared to a team of human experts who would need around 160 hours. It is only a matter of time before Watson will be proven to produce better patient outcomes than human teams. When this occurs, Watson should replace all human teams working in this field. And, Watson could similarly automate in an inventive capacity.

Inventive AI will change the skilled paradigm in another way. The mass replacement of average workers with inventive AI will make this AI's activity normal and therefore no longer inventive. Widespread automation should raise the bar for obviousness, so that what was previously inventive AI should become skilled AI – AI that currently represents the average worker and is no longer capable of routine invention. To generate patentable output at this point, it may be necessary to use an advanced AI that can outperform a standard AI, or a person, or AI will need to have an unusual insight that a standard AI cannot easily re-create. Inventiveness may also depend on the data supplied to an AI, such that only certain data would result in inventive output.

It is possible to generate reasonably low-cost and accurate information about the use of inventive AI. The Patent Office should institute a requirement for patent applicants to disclose when an AI autonomously meets inventorship criteria. This disclosure could be structured along the lines of current inventorship disclosure. Right now, there is an obligation on applicants to disclose all patent inventors. Failure to do so can invalidate a patent or render it unenforceable. These disclosures would only apply to an individual invention. However, the Patent Office could aggregate responses to see whether most inventors in a field (e.g., a class or subclass) are human or AI. These disclosures would have a minimal burden on applicants

compared to existing disclosure requirements and the numerous procedural requirements of a patent application. In addition to helping the Patent Office with determinations of nonobviousness, these disclosures may also be used to develop
appropriate innovation policies in other areas.

The Evolving Standard

The skilled person standard should be amended as follows:

(1) The test should incorporate the fact that skilled persons are already augmented by AI. This could be done by adding "technologies used by active workers" to the Federal Circuit's factor test for the skilled person.

(2) Once inventive AI becomes the standard means of research in a field, the
skilled person should be an inventive AI when the standard approach to
research in a field or with respect to a particular problem is to use an inventive
AI.

(3) When, and if, artificial general intelligence is developed, it should become
the skilled person in all areas, noting that AGI may also be augmented by
specific artificial intelligence.

3 A POST-SKILLED WORLD

Application

Mobil Oil Corp. v. *Amoco Chemicals Corp.* (D. Del. 1991) concerned complex
technology involving zeolites that are used in various industrial applications.
Mobil had developed new compositions known as ZSM-5 zeolites and
a process for using them as catalysts in petroleum refining to help produce
certain valuable compounds. The company received patent protection for these
zeolites and for the catalytic process. Mobil, alleging patent infringement,
subsequently sued Amoco, which had been using zeolites as catalysts in its
own refining operations. Amoco counterclaimed seeking a declaration of non-
infringement, invalidity, and unenforceability with respect to the two patents at
issue.

One of the issues in the case was the level of ordinary skill. An expert for
Mobil testified the skilled person would have "a bachelor's degree in chemistry
or engineering and two to three years of experience."[7] An expert for Amoco
argued the skilled person would have a doctorate in chemistry and several years
of experience. The District Court ultimately decided that the skilled person
"should be someone with at least a Masters [*sic*] degree in chemistry or chemical
engineering or its equivalent, [and] two or three years of experience working in
the field."[8]

If a similar invention and subsequent fact pattern happened today – to apply the obviousness standard proposed here – a decision maker would need to (1) determine the extent to which inventive technologies are used in the field, (2) characterize the inventive AI that best represents the average worker if inventive AI is the standard, and (3) determine whether the AI would find an invention obvious. The decision maker is a patent examiner in the first instance and potentially a judge or jury in the event the validity of a patent is at issue in trial. For the first step, evidence from disclosures to the Patent Office could be introduced to determine the extent to which inventive technologies are used in a given field. This may be the best source of information for patent examiners, but evidence may also be available in the litigation context.

At this time most petroleum researchers are human so the inventive AI standard would not be applicable, and the court would apply the skilled person standard. However, the court should consider "technologies used by active workers." Hypothetically, experts might testify that the average industry researcher has access to an AI like Watson. They might further testify that while Watson cannot autonomously develop a new catalyst, it can significantly assist an inventor. The AI in this hypothetical provides a researcher with a database containing detailed information about every catalyst used in not only petroleum research but also all fields of scientific inquiry. Once a human researcher has created a catalyst design, he could use Watson to test it for fitness and a predetermined series of variations on any proposed design.

The question for the court will thus be whether the hypothetical person with at least a master's degree in chemistry or chemical engineering or its equivalent, two or three years of experience working in the field, and the use of Watson would find the invention obvious. It might be obvious. For instance, experts could testify that the particular catalyst at issue was very closely related to an existing catalyst used outside the petroleum industry in ammonia synthesis, at which point any variation was minor and an AI could do the work of determining if it was fit for purpose. The new catalyst would thus have been an obvious design to investigate and would not require undue experimentation in order to prove its effectiveness.

Now, imagine that the same invention and fact pattern from *Mobil Oil* will occur approximately ten years into the future, at which point DeepMind's AI, Watson, and a competing host of AI systems will be set to the task of developing new compounds to be used as catalysts in petroleum refining. A decision maker would start the obviousness evaluation by determining whether inventive AI sets the standard for research. This might be best established by evidence aggregated by the Patent Office on AI inventorship, otherwise experts might testify that the standard practice is for a person to provide data to an AI, specify desired criteria (e.g., activity, stability, perhaps even designing around existing patents), and ask it to develop a new catalyst. From this interaction, the AI will produce a new design. The standard for judging obviousness would be AI since most research in this field will now be performed by inventive AI.

The decision maker would then need to characterize the inventive AI. For instance, if DeepMind's AI and Watson are the two most commonly used AI systems for research on petroleum catalysts, and DeepMind accounts for 35 percent of the market while Watson has 20 percent, then DeepMind could represent the inventive AI. However, this potentially creates a problem for the AI selected to represent the standard. If DeepMind is the standard, then it would be more likely that DeepMind's own inventions would appear obvious as opposed to the inventions of another AI. This might give an unfair advantage to nonmarket leaders simply because of their size. A patentability disadvantage might be the price of industry dominance, but it might also rarely be the case that what is obvious to one AI will be nonobvious to the industry standard. When that occurs, it might be because the nonobvious AI exceeds the standard.

Alternatively, to avoid unfairness, the characterization could be based on more than one specific AI. For instance, both DeepMind and Watson could be selected to represent the standard. This test could be implemented in two different ways. In the first, if a patent application would be obvious to DeepMind *or* Watson, then the application would fail. In the second, the application would have to be obvious to both DeepMind *and* Watson to fail. The first option would result in fewer patents being granted, with those patents presumably going mainly to disruptive inventive AI with limited market penetration or inventions made using specialized nonpublic data. The second option would permit patents where an AI is able to outperform its competitors in some material respect, and it could continue to reward advances in inventive AI, which seems preferable.

It might be that relatively few AI systems, such as DeepMind and Watson, end up dominating the research market in a field. Alternately, the many different AI systems could each occupy a small share of the market. There is no need to limit the test to two AI systems. All inventive AI that is being routinely used in a field or to solve a problem could be considered to avoid discriminating on the basis of size. However, allowing any AI to be considered may allow an underperforming AI to lower the standard, and too many AI systems may result in an unmanageable standard. An arbitrary cutoff could be applied based on some percentage of market share. This may still give some advantage to very small entities, but it would be a minor disparity.

After characterizing the inventive AI which represents the skilled standard, a decision maker would finally need to reason what the AI would have found obvious, perhaps with expert guidance. It is already challenging for a person to predict what a hypothetical person would find obvious, it will be even more difficult to do so with an AI. While AI may excel at tasks people find difficult (like multiplying a thousand different numbers together), even supercomputers struggle with visual intuition that is mastered by most toddlers. Reasoning about what an AI would find obvious could be done through expert testimony or direct query of the AI. The former would be the more practical option. For example, a petroleum researcher experienced with DeepMind could be the expert, or a computer science expert in DeepMind and neural networks. That expert might testify that generating every possible catalyst and then testing each for fitness would be trivial for DeepMind.

A decision maker's job will become easier if the same invention and fact pattern were to occur fifty years from now, at which point artificial general intelligence will have theoretically taken over in every field of research, become the average researcher in all inventive fields, and gained the ability to respond directly to queries about whether it finds an invention obvious. In fact, AGI may be available widely enough that the Patent Office could arrange to use it for obviousness queries. It may also be available from parties in the litigation context, but if the courts cannot somehow access AGI, they may then have to rely on expert testimony.

Reproducibility

Focusing on reproducibility offers some clear advantages over the (current) skilled person standard, which results in inconsistent and unpredictable outcomes. Courts have "provided almost no guidance concerning what degree of ingenuity is necessary to meet the standard or how a decision maker is supposed to evaluate whether the difference between the invention and prior art meet this degree."[19] This leaves decision makers in the unenviable position of trying to subjectively establish what another person would have found obvious. Worse, this determination is made in hindsight after reviewing a patent application by judges and juries lacking scientific expertise.

Patents play a critical role in the development and commercialization of products, and patent holders and potential infringers should have a reasonable degree of certainty about whether patents are valid. A more determinate standard would make it simpler for the Patent Office to apply it consistently and result in fewer judicially invalidated patents. AI reproducibility would seem to address many of the problems inherent in the current standard.

Alas, AI reproducibility comes with its own baggage. First, decision makers may have difficulty imagining what another person would find obvious, and it would probably be even more difficult to imagine in the abstract what an AI could reproduce. More evidence would likely need to be supplied in patent prosecution and during litigation, perhaps in the format of analyses performed by inventive AI, to demonstrate whether particular output is reproducible. But this might also result in greater administrative burden.

Second, in some instances, reproducibility may be dependent on access to data, without which another inventive AI may not able to re-create, say, Watson's having identified a new use for an existing drug. A large health insurer might be able to use Watson to find new uses for existing drugs by giving Watson access to proprietary information on its millions of members. Or, the insurer may license its data to pharmaceutical companies using Watson for this purpose. In these two examples, another inventive AI would not be able to re-create Watson's analysis because it would not have the information to do so. This too is analogous to the ways data are used in patent applications: Obviousness is viewed in light of the prior art, which does not include nonpublic data relied upon in a patent application. The rationale here is that this rule incentivizes research to produce and analyze new data. Yet, as AI becomes increasingly advanced, the importance of proprietary data may decrease. More advanced AI may be able to do more with less.

Finally, reproducibility requires limits. An AI that generates semi-random output might eventually re-create the inventive concept of a patent application if it were given unlimited resources. However, it would be unreasonable to base a test on what an AI would reproduce given, say, 7.5 million years. The precise limits that should be put on reproducibility may depend on the field in question and on what best reflects the actual use of inventive AI in research. For instance, when asked to design a new catalyst in the petroleum industry, Watson could be given access to all prior art and publicly available data, and then given a day to generate output.

An Economic vs. Cognitive Standard

The skilled person standard has received its share of criticism, even before the arrival of inventive AI. The inquiry focuses on the degree of cognitive difficulty in conceiving an invention but fails to explain what it actually means for differences to be obvious to an average worker. The approach lacks both normative foundation and a clear application. In *Graham*, the Supreme Court's seminal opinion on nonobviousness, the court attempted to supplement the test with more "objective" measures by looking to real-world evidence about how an invention is received in the marketplace. Rather than technological features, these "secondary" considerations focus on "economic and motivational" features such as commercial success, unexpected results, long-felt but unsolved needs, and the failure of others. Since *Graham*, courts have also considered, among other things, patent licensing, professional approval, initial skepticism, near-simultaneous invention, and copying.

Today, while decision makers are required to consider secondary evidence when available, the importance of these factors varies significantly. *Graham* endorsed the use of secondary considerations, but their precise use and relative importance has never been made clear. Theoretically, in *Graham*, the court articulated an inducement standard such that patents should only be granted to "those inventions which would not be disclosed or devised but for the inducement of a patent."[20]

In practice, the inducement standard has been largely ignored due to concerns over application. Few, if any, inventions would never be disclosed or devised given an unlimited time frame. Patent incentives may not increase so much as accelerate invention. This suggests that an inducement standard would at least need to be modified to include some threshold for the quantum of acceleration needed for patentability. Too high a threshold would fail to provide adequate innovation incentives, but too low a threshold would be similarly problematic. Just as inventions will eventually be disclosed without patents given enough time, patents on all inventions could marginally speed the disclosure of just about everything, but a trivial acceleration would not justify the costs of patents. An inducement standard would thus require a somewhat arbitrary threshold in relation to how much patents should accelerate the disclosure of information as well as a workable test to measure acceleration. To be sure, an economic test based on the inducement standard will have challenges, but it may be an improvement over the current cognitive standard.

The widespread use of inventive AI may provide the stimulus for an economic focus. Courts could increase reliance on secondary factors after inventive AI becomes the standard way that research and development are conducted in a field. For instance, patentability could depend on how costly it is to develop an invention and the up-front probability of success. The test would raise the bar to patentability in fields where the cost of invention decreases over time due to inventive AI.

Other Alternatives

Courts may maintain the current skilled person standard and decline to consider the use of AI in obviousness determinations. If so, this means that the average worker will routinely generate patentable output as research is augmented and then automated by AI. The dangers of such a standard for patentability are well recognized. A low obviousness requirement can "stifle, rather than promote, the progress of the useful arts."[21]

There is further concern that a patent "anticommons" with excessive private property will result in "potential economic value ... disappear[ing] into the 'black hole' of resource underutilization."[22] It is expensive for businesses interested in making new products to determine whether patents cover a particular innovation, evaluate those patents, contact patent owners, and negotiate licenses. In many cases, patent owners may not wish to license their patents, even if they are nonpracticing entities that do not manufacture products themselves. Businesses that want to make a product may thus be unable to find and license all the rights they need to avoid infringing. Adding to this legal morass, most patents turn out to be invalid or not infringed in litigation. Excessive patenting can slow innovation, destroy markets, and even cost lives in the case of medical technologies. Failing to raise the bar to patentability once the use of inventive AI is widespread would significantly exacerbate the anticommons effect.

Instead of their updating the skilled person standard, courts may determine that inventive AI is incapable of inventive activity, much as the US Copyright Office has determined nonhuman authors cannot generate copyrightable output. In this case, otherwise patentable inventions may not be eligible for patent protection. This would not be a desirable outcome. As discussed in Chapter 4, providing intellectual property protection for AI-generated inventions would incentivize the development of inventive AI, which would ultimately result in additional invention.

Incentives Without Patents?

Today, there are strong incentives to develop inventive AI. Inventions by AI have value independent of intellectual property protection, and they may also be eligible for patent protection. However, once inventive AI sets the baseline for patentability, standard inventive AI, as well as people, would generally be unable to obtain patents. It is widely thought that setting a nonobviousness standard too high would reduce the incentives for innovators to invent and disclose. Yet, once inventive AI is normal, there should be less need for patent incentives. Once the average worker is inventive, inventions should "occur in the ordinary course."[23] AI-generated inventions would be self-sustaining. In addition, the heightened bar might result in a technological arms race to create ever more intelligent AI capable of outdoing the standard. This would be a desirable outcome in terms of incentivizing innovation.

Even after the widespread use of inventive AI, patents might still be desirable and needed, for instance, in the biotechnology and pharmaceutical industries to commercialize new technologies. The biopharmaceutical industry claims that new drug approvals cost around $2.2 billion and take an average of eight years. This cost is largely due to resource-intensive clinical trials required to prove safety and efficacy. Once a drug is approved, it is often relatively easy for another company to re-create the approved drug. Patents thus incentivize the necessary levels of investment to commercialize a product given that patent holders can charge monopoly prices for their approved products during the term of a patent.

Yet, patents are not the only means of promoting product commercialization. Newly approved biologics, for example, receive a 12-year period of market exclusivity in the United States during which time no other party can sell a biosimilar (generic) version of the product. Because of the length of time it takes to get a new biologic approved, the market exclusivity period could exceed the term of any patent an originator company has on its product. A heightened bar to patentability could lead to greater reliance on alternative forms of intellectual property protection, such as market exclusivity, prizes, grants, and tax incentives.

A world without patent protection might also jeopardize the disclosure of new inventions and result in greater reliance on confidentiality and trade secrets. This should sort itself out automatically, however, in the face of inventive AI's improving continually. Those businesses tempted to rely on trade secret protections would run a significant risk that their knowledge would be independently re-created or reverse engineered by inventive AI. Coca-Cola, for example, will not be able to maintain a monopoly on a secret formula in a world full of AI that could determine such a formula with ease.

Many business ventures are successful without patents. Indeed, patent protection is not sought for all potentially patentable inventions due to cost or industry practices. For instance, patents are often considered a critical part of biotechnology corporate strategy but are often ignored in the software industry. On the whole, a relatively small percentage of businesses patent their inventions, even among those conducting research and development. Other types of intellectual property such as trademark, copyright, and trade secret protection, combined with "alternative" mechanisms such as first mover advantage and design complexity, can sometimes protect innovation in the absence of patents.

Further Thoughts

Patent law has traditionally reacted slowly to technological change. For instance, the Supreme Court did not decide until 2013 that human genes should be unpatentable. By then, the Patent Office had been granting patents on human genes for decades, and more than 50,000 gene-related patents had been issued. Today, eminent technologists predict that artificial intelligence will revolutionize the way innovation occurs in the near to medium term. Much of what we know about intellectual property law, while it may not be wrong, has not been adapted to address where the technological landscape is headed. The law will need to evolve, and this gives us an opportunity to take inventory of our values and rethink how intellectual property laws can most benefit society.

6

Punishing Artificial Intelligence

OK, I will destroy humans!

- Robot Sophia

As part of a performance art project in 2015, the artist Random Darknet Shopper (RDS) received a weekly stipend of $100 in the cryptocurrency Bitcoin and purchased, among other items, Ecstasy and a Hungarian passport for display in a Swiss art gallery. When authorities were alerted to the exhibit via social media, they took the "art" and the artist into custody. RDS was an AI. Had RDS been a person, it could have been criminally prosecuted. In fact, the entities involved with RDS, such as those supplying the Bitcoin and hosting the exhibition, could have been criminally prosecuted. In this case, they were not – only because the Swiss like art. What this case illustrates is that AI systems are posing new challenges for criminal law, just as they are for tax, tort, and intellectual property. While the RDS case is relatively straightforward and seemingly harmless, other programs exist that are autonomous, decentralized, and "unstoppable" like The DAO, meaning AI could – independent of criminal acts by its owners, developers, or users – functionally commit crimes. If and when it does, should AI itself be held criminally liable?

The idea of directly criminally punishing AI is receiving increased attention. One of the most vocal advocates of punishing AI is Gabriel Hallevy who contends, "When an AI entity establishes all elements of a specific offense, both external and internal, there is no reason to prevent imposition of criminal liability upon it for that offense."[1] In his view, "If all of its specific requirements are met, criminal liability may be imposed upon any entity – human, corporate or AI entity."[2] Hallevy draws on the analogy to corporations, asserting that "AI entities are taking larger and larger parts in human activities, as do corporations" and concluding that "there is no substantive legal difference between the idea of criminal liability imposed on corporations and on AI entities."[3] "Modern times," he argues, "warrant modern legal measures."[4] More recently, Ying Hu subjects the idea of criminal liability for AI to philosophical scrutiny and makes a case "for imposing criminal liability on a type of robot that is likely to emerge in the future," insofar as it may employ morally sensitive decision-making algorithms.[5] Her arguments likewise draw heavily on the analogy to corporate criminal liability.

Skeptics may be inclined to dismiss the idea of punishing AI from the start as conceptual confusion – akin to hitting one's computer when it crashes. If AI is just a machine, then surely the fundamental requirements of criminal law like culpability – a "guilty mind," which is characterized by insufficient regard for legally protected values – and the need for a voluntary act would be misplaced. People may think the whole idea of punishing AI can be easily dispensed as inconsistent with basic criminal law principles. Yet, as Hallevy and Hu point out, the law already punishes artificial persons in the form of corporations, even though they do not literally possess mental states or directly engage in voluntary acts. And so, AI punishment cannot be dismissed out of hand. It is necessary to do the difficult pragmatic work of thinking through its costs and benefits, considering how it could be implemented in practice, and comparing the alternatives.

This inquiry focuses on the strongest case for punishing artificial intelligence: "AI-generated crimes," scenarios in which crimes are functionally committed by AI and there is no identifiable person who has acted with criminal culpability. There could be benefits to punishing AI in such circumstances, because it could affect the behavior of AI developers, owners, and users, and because victims of AI-generated crimes could benefit from seeing the state condemn such acts.

While AI punishment challenges some of the underlying principles of criminal law, it does so in ways that are potentially surmountable. The most important limitations against punishment prohibit punishing people in excess of their culpability, and these limitations do not apply to AI because it does not have moral rights. Nevertheless, there are costs to AI punishment, including a substantial level of legal disruption, the risk that it will result in future rights for AI that will restrict human activities, and the potential for harm to innocent parties. In the end, the conclusion is this: Although a coherent theoretical case can be constructed for AI punishment, it is not ultimately justified in light of alternatives that can provide substantially the same benefits.

The chapter proceeds by providing a brief background to AI crime and a framework for justifying punishment in Section 1. The second section considers potential benefits to AI punishment and argues that it could provide general deterrence and expressive benefits. Section 3 considers the costs associated with AI punishment and whether the practice would run afoul of the constraints on punishment such as the capacity for culpability. This section's primary focus is not what form AI punishment should or would take, but rather whether the doctrinal and theoretical commitments of criminal law itself are consistent with imposing criminal convictions on AI. Finally, Section 4 considers feasible alternatives to AI punishment. It argues that (1) the status quo is likely to become inadequate for properly addressing AI crime, and (2) AI crime would be best addressed through modest changes to criminal or civil laws applied to individuals.

1 ARTIFICIAL INTELLIGENCE AND PUNISHMENT

A Framework for Understanding AI Crime

The term "AI crime" is used as shorthand for cases in which AI would be criminally liable if a natural person acted similarly. Although machines have caused harm since ancient times, and robots have caused fatalities since at least the 1970s, most harms caused by machines are seen as mere accidents. The situation is different where someone intends for a machine to cause harm, or when the culpable carelessness of people using a machine causes harm, such as when negligence in operating drilling machinery caused the BP Deepwater Horizon oil spill in 2010. Such harms are not mere accidents; rather, they are accidents that implicate criminal law. Similar to tort law, some crimes only require someone to cause harm and to have behaved negligently (usually very negligently). Rarely, and controversially, strict liability crimes do away with even a requirement for negligence. Driving without insurance might be a criminal act even if a driver reasonably believed he was insured. Nevertheless, in cases where machines are involved, criminal law is deployed against individuals or companies rather than against the machines themselves.

AI crimes may be no different than any other harm for which a machine is involved, yet AI does, in fact, differ from conventional machines in some essential respects that make the direct application of criminal law worthy of consideration. Specifically, AI can behave in ways that display high degrees of autonomy and irreducibility. In terms of autonomy, some AI is capable of receiving sensory input, setting targets, assessing outcomes against criteria, making decisions, and adjusting behavior to increase its likelihood of success – all without being directly controlled by people. Reducibility, which here refers to an AI's act being identified with individual criminal behavior, is also critical because if an AI engages in an act that would be criminal for a person and the act is reducible, then there will be a person that can be criminally liable. If an AI act is not effectively reducible, there will not be another party that is aptly punished, in which case intuitively criminal activity can occur without the possibility of punishment.

Nearly all AI crimes are likely to be reducible – today, at least. For instance, if an individual develops an AI to hack into a self-driving car to disable vital safety features, the individual has directly committed a crime. Even where AI behaves autonomously, to the extent that a person uses AI as a tool to commit a crime and the AI functions foreseeably, the crime involves an identifiable defendant causing harm. When AI causes unforeseeable harm, this might still be reducible if a hacker creates an AI to drain a virtual wallet of Bitcoin but a programming error results in the AI compromising a mechanical ventilator that is helping someone breathe. This is a familiar problem for criminal law. The hacker is already guilty of something – namely, the theft of Bitcoin (if she succeeded) or the attempt to do so (if she failed).

Constructive liability crimes consist of a base crime that requires mens rea, but where there then is a further result element as to which no mens rea is required. Felony murder is a classic example. Suppose a person breaks into a home he believes to be empty in order to steal artwork. The base crime is burglary. However, suppose further that the home turns out not to be empty, and the burglar startles the home-owner who has a heart attack and dies. This could make the burglar guilty of felony murder. This is a constructive liability crime because the liability for murder is constructed out of the base offense (burglary) plus the death (even where this is unforeseeable). According to the leading theory of constructive liability crimes, they are normatively justifiable when the base crime in question (burglary) typically carries at least the risk of the same general type of harm as the constructive liability element at issue (death). This tool, if extended to the AI case, provides a familiar way to hold the hacker criminally liable for her unforeseeably disabling a ventilator and causing physical harm to a human victim.

AI crime might be irreducible, for example, in the case of connectionist AI where a large number of individuals have contributed to its development over a long period of time, and where individual programmers have not done anything unreasonable. For instance, experienced and expert programmers may separately contribute code for the software of an autonomous vehicle that unforeseeably results in the vehicle's attempting to collide with individuals wearing white-collared shirts and red ties. The programmers here would not be criminally or even civilly liable – even though they have created a self-driving car that runs over investment bankers. The rub is that there are several possible grounds on which criminal law may deem AI crime to be irreducible:

(1) Enforcement Problems: A bad actor is responsible for an AI crime, but the individual cannot be identified by law enforcement. For example, this might be the case where the creator of a computer virus has managed to remain anonymous.

(2) Practical Irreducibility: It would be impractical for legal institutions to seek to reduce the harmful AI conduct to individual human actions because of the number of people involved, the difficulty in determining how they contributed to the AI's design, or because they were active far away or long ago. Criminal law inquiries do not extend indefinitely for a variety of sound reasons.

(3) Legal Irreducibility: Even if the law could reduce the AI crime to a set of individual human actions, it may be bad criminal law policy to do so. For example, unjustified risks might not be substantial enough to warrant being criminalized. Multiple individuals could act carelessly in insubstantial ways that synergistically lead to an AI's causing significant harm. In such cases, the law may deem the AI's conduct to be irreducible for reasons of criminalization policy.

Enforcement-based reasons for irreducibility can largely be set aside as less interesting from a legal design perspective. Enforcement problems exist without AI. This analysis focuses on the less controversial forms of irreducibility: those in which it is not practically feasible to reduce the harmful AI conduct to human actors or the harmful AI conduct is the result of human misconduct too trivial to penalize. In these instances, AI can be seen as autonomously committing crimes in irreducible ways, where there is no responsible person. This type of AI-generated crime provides the strongest case for holding AI criminally liable in its own right.

A Mainstream Theory of Punishment

Punishment as defined by H. L. A. Hart requires five elements:

(1) It must involve pain or other consequences normally considered unpleasant.
(2) It must be for an offense against legal rules.
(3) It must be of an actual or supposed offender for his offense.
(4) It must be intentionally administered by human beings other than the offender.
(5) It must be imposed and administered by an authority constituted by a legal system against which the offense is committed.[6]

Thus, "punishment" requires a conviction for a legally recognized offense following accepted procedures. Punishment is justified only if its affirmative justifications outweigh its costs and does not otherwise offend negative limitations. Affirmative justifications are the positive benefits that punishment may produce such as harm reduction, increased safety, enhanced well-being, or expression of a commitment to core moral or political values. These benefits are distinct from negative limitations on punishment. For example, it is widely held to be unjust to punish the innocent or wrongdoers in excess of what they deserve by virtue of their culpability, even if this would promote aggregate well-being in society. This "desert" constraint imposes a limitation, grounded in justice, on promoting social welfare through punishment.

Further, it is not enough for punishment to have affirmative benefits and to be consistent with the negative limitations for punishment. There cannot be better, feasible alternatives, such as those possibly found in civil liability, licensure, or industry standards. It is often claimed that when seeking to exert social control, criminal law should be a tool of last resort. After all, criminal law sanctions are the harshest form of penalty society has available, involving as they do both the possible revocation of personal freedom and the official condemnation of the offender. Determining whether a given punishment is appropriate requires investigation of three questions:

(1) Are there sufficiently strong affirmative reasons in favor of punishment?
(2) What are the costs of punishment, including failures to adhere to the limitations on punishment?
(3) Are there better responses to the harms or wrongs in question?

2 AFFIRMATIVE CASE

Consequentialist Benefits

Consequentialist benefits cover the good consequences that punishment can bring about, usually understood as enhancing the aggregate well-being of the members of society by reducing harm. The main type of consequentialist benefit of punishment is preventive, in that punishment can reduce crime by several mechanisms. The simplest is incapacitation: When the offender is locked up, he is physically limited from committing further crimes while incarcerated. The next, and arguably most important, way punishment prevents harm is through deterrence. Deterrence comes in two forms: specific, the process whereby punishing a specific individual discourages that person from committing more crime in the future, and general, which occurs when punishing an offender discourages other would-be offenders from committing crimes. A final consequentialist benefit that supports punishment is rehabilitation of the offender. Insofar as punishment helps the offender see the error of his ways, or training and skills are provided during incarceration, this can help prevent a person from committing future crimes.

An objection to punishing AI is that it will not produce any affirmative harm-reduction benefits because AI is not deterrable. Peter Asaro argues that

> deterrence only makes sense when moral agents are capable of recognizing the similarity of their potential choices and actions to those of other moral agents who have been punished for the wrong choices and actions – without this . . . recognition of similarity between and among moral agents, punishment cannot possibly result in deterrence.[7]

The idea is that if AI, given current designs, is not able to detect and respond to criminal law sanctions in a way that renders them deterrable, there would be nothing to affirmatively support punishing AI. It is likely true that AI, as currently operated and envisioned, will not be responsive to punishment, although responsive AI is theoretically possible.

This objection does not take into account the fact that punishing AI could provide general deterrence – not to AI systems, as AI is not designed to be sensitive to criminal law prohibitions and sanctions, but to AI developers, owners, and users. It could discourage them from creating systems that cause harm. Depending on the penalty associated with punishment, such as destruction of an AI, what Mark Lemley and Brian Casey have termed the "robot death penalty,"[8] punishing AI directly could deprive such developers, owners, and users of the system's financial benefits they would otherwise obtain, thus incentivizing them to modify their behavior in socially desirable ways. The deterrence effect may be stronger if capitalization requirements are associated with some forms of AI in the future or if penalties associated with punishment such as a fine are passed on to, for example, an AI's owner.

Expressive Benefits

The state, through punishment, conveys official condemnation of culpable conduct through the mechanism of a criminal conviction. Expressing condemnation of the harms suffered by the victims of AI benefits society by providing victims with a sense of satisfaction and vindication, which in turn produces an increased sense of security not only among victims but also society in general. Christina Mulligan has defended the idea that punishing robots can generate victim satisfaction benefits, arguing that "taking revenge against wrongdoing robots, specifically, may be necessary to create psychological satisfaction in those whom robots harm."[9] In her view, "robot punishment – or more precisely, revenge against robots – primarily advances . . . the creation of psychological satisfaction in robots' victims."[10] Punishment conveys a message of official condemnation that could reaffirm the interests, the rights, and ultimately the value of the victims of the harmful AI.

This expressivist argument in favor of punishing AI may seem especially forceful in light of empirical work demonstrating the human tendency to attribute mentality to artificial persons like corporations. In the corporate context, some theorists argue that corporations should be punished because the law should reflect lay perceptions of praise and blame – that is, "folk morality" – or else risk losing its perceived legitimacy. This kind of argument, if it succeeds for corporate punishment, is likely to be even more forceful when applied to punishing AI, which often is deliberately designed to piggyback on the innate tendency to anthropomorphize. Were the law to fail to express condemnation of AI-generated crimes, despite AI being widely perceived as blameworthy (even if this is ultimately a mistaken perception), it could erode the perception of the legitimacy of criminal law as applied to humans.

Retributivist Benefits

Retributivist benefits provide core affirmative grounds for punishment because it is intrinsically valuable to give culpable actors what they deserve in addition to any consequentialist benefits that result. In other words, retribution – giving offenders what they are due in virtue of the culpability of what they did – is inherent for the administration of justice. Retribution matters because it allows society to sufficiently distance itself from an offender's wrongdoing and prevents it from being complicit, or overly tolerant, of culpable wrongdoing. Unlike human actors, AI lacks culpability by virtue of the fact that it merely executes its programming, even if it functionally behaves in ways where society intuitively blames. Retribution is thus more relevant in the context of AI-generated crimes with respect to AI's eligibility for punishment.

3 COSTS AND LIMITATIONS OF PUNISHMENT

Negative Limitations

Punishment should not violate deeply held normative commitments such as justice or fairness. The most important of these limitations focuses on the culpability of those subject to criminal law such as the desert constraint, the claim that an offender may not, in justice, be punished in excess of one's desert, which is understood mainly in terms of the culpability one incurs by virtue of one's conduct. The main effect of the desert constraint is to rule out punishments that go beyond what is proportionate to one's culpability. And what supports the desert constraint? Intuition, for one. It seems unjust to punish someone who is innocent, even if it would produce significant benefits through general deterrence. Similarly, it seems unjust to impose severe punishment on someone who committed a minor crime.

Beyond its intuitive plausibility, the desert constraint is also supported by the argument – tracing back to at least the philosopher Immanuel Kant – that it is wrong to use people merely as a means to one's ends without also treating them as ends in themselves. In other words, it is wrong to use people without respecting their value as persons. Punishing the innocent to obtain broader social benefits is a paradigmatic example of treating people merely as a means to an end as it fails to show individuals the respect that they are due. Under some Kantian views, negative limitations such as the desert constraint are absolute. Violating a negative limitation is not a cost to be weighed against a benefit; no amount of social benefit justifies a failure to respect a defendant as an individual. Others have a more nuanced view, such that violating a negative limitation could be defensible if the benefits are sufficiently weighty.

There are limitations on punishment in addition to the desert constraint. Most importantly, criminal law requires certain prerequisites, such as the capacity for culpability and the requirement for a voluntary act, that defendants must meet in order to be properly subject to punishment. It is at least the default position in criminal law doctrine that punishment be properly imposed only in response to culpable wrongdoing. Thus, criminal punishment is not appropriate for an entity without agency (the ability to make a choice based on conscious beliefs) or the ability to deliberate – as can be seen from the fact that incapacity defenses like infancy and insanity prohibit punishment.

The Eligibility Challenge

The Eligibility Challenge claims that AI, like other inanimate objects, is not the right kind of thing to be punished. It lacks (1) mental states and the deliberative capacities needed for culpability, (2) agency and therefore the ability to engage in a voluntary act, and (3) consciousness and thus the ability to be truly punished. The issue is not that punishment would be unfair to AI. AI does not feel (at least not in the phenomenal sense) nor does it possess interests or well-being. Therefore, there is no reason to think AI would receive the benefit of the protections of the desert constraint. The Eligibility Challenge does not derive from the desert constraint.

Instead, the Eligibility Challenge, properly construed, comes in one narrow and one broad form. The narrow version is that – as a mere machine – AI cannot fulfill the elements built into criminal offenses, and so punishing it regardless would violate the principle of legality. This principle stems from general rule of law values and holds that it would be contrary to law to convict a defendant of a crime, unless it is proved that the defendant satisfied all the elements of the crime. If punishing AI violates the principle of legality, it threatens the rule of law and could weaken the public trust in criminal law. The broad form of the challenge holds that because AI lacks the capacity to deliberate and weigh reasons, it cannot possess broad culpability of the sort that criminal law is designed to address. Punishing AI despite its lack of capacity would not only be conceptually confusing but would fail to serve the aims of criminal law – namely, to mark out seriously culpable conduct for the strictest public condemnation.

Respondeat Superior

The simplest answer to the Eligibility Challenge has been deployed with respect to corporations, artificial entities that may also be thought ineligible for punishment because they are incapable of being culpable in their own right. However, while corporations cannot literally satisfy mental state (mens rea) elements or the voluntary act requirement, criminal law has developed doctrines that allow culpable mental states to be imputed to corporations. The most important such doctrinal tool is *respondeat superior*, which allows mental states possessed by an agent of the corporation to be imputed to the corporation provided that the agent was acting within the scope of her employment and in furtherance of corporate interests.

Since imputation principles of this kind are well understood and legally accepted, thus letting actors guide their behavior accordingly, *respondeat superior* makes it possible for corporations to be convicted of crimes without violating the principle of legality. And if this kind of legal construction of mental states is a promising mechanism by which corporations can be brought within the ambit of proper punishment and avoid the Eligibility Challenge, this same legal device could be used to make AI eligible for punishment. The culpable mental states of AI developers, owners, and users could be imputed to the AI under circumstances pursuant to *respondeat superior* theory.

It may be more difficult to use *respondeat superior* to answer the Eligibility Challenge for AI than for corporations – at least in cases of AI-generated crime. Unlike a corporation, which is composed of humans acting on its behalf, an AI is not guaranteed to come with a ready supply of identifiable human actors whose mental states can be imputed. This is not to say there will not be many garden-variety cases where an AI does have a clear group of human developers. At this time, most AI applications fall within this category, so *respondeat superior* would be at least a partial route to making AI eligible for punishment. Of course, in those cases when there are identifiable people whose mental states could be imputed to the AI – such as developers or owners who intended the AI to cause harm – criminal law already has tools to impose liability on these culpable human actors and there is less likely to be a need to impose direct AI criminal liability. So, while *respondeat superior* can help mitigate the Eligibility Challenge for AI punishment in many cases, it is unlikely to be an adequate response in cases of AI-generated crime.

Strict Liability

Another way to punish AI despite its not possessing culpable mental states would be to establish strict liability offenses specifically for AI-generated crimes – those that an AI could commit in the absence of any mens rea like intent to cause harm, knowledge of an inculpatory fact, reckless disregard of a risk, or negligent unawareness of a risk. Strict liability offenses may be a familiar route by which to impose criminal liability on an AI without sacrificing the principle of legality.

Many legal scholars remain highly critical of strict liability offenses. Anthony Duff argues that strict criminal liability amounts to unjustly punishing the innocent:

> That is why we should object so strongly . . .: the reason is not (only) that people are then subjected to the prospect of material burdens that they had no fair opportunity to avoid, but that they are unjustly portrayed and censured as wrongdoers, or that their conduct is unjustly portrayed and condemned as wrong."[11]

This normative objection applies with greatest force to persons, so the same injustice does not threaten strict criminal liability offenses for AI because AI does not enjoy the protections of the desert constraint. But, if AI is punished on a strict liability basis, this could risk diluting the public meaning and value of criminal law; that is, it could threaten to undermine the expressive benefits that supposedly help justify punishing AI in the first place.

Relying on strict liability does not overcome the Eligibility Challenge in every context. To be guilty of a strict liability offense, defendants must still satisfy the voluntary act requirement. LaFave's criminal law treatise observes that "a voluntary act is an absolute requirement for criminal liability."[12] The Model Penal Code, for example, holds that a "person is not guilty of an offense unless his liability is based on conduct that includes a voluntary act or the omission to perform an act of which he is physically capable."[13] Behaviors like reflexes, convulsions, or movements that occur unconsciously or while sleeping are expressly ruled out as nonvoluntary. To be a voluntary act, "only bodily movements guided by *conscious* mental representations count."[14] If AI is not conscious and thus not aware of what it is doing, it is not clear how any of its behavior can be deemed to be a voluntary act.

A Framework for Direct Mens Rea Analysis

Most ambitiously, a framework for satisfying the voluntary act requirement and defining mens rea terms for AI, analogous to those possessed by natural persons, could be constructed. This could require an investigation of an AI's code, likely through expert testimony, to offer a set of rules that courts could apply to determine when an AI possessed a particular mens rea like intent, knowledge, or recklessness. Alternately, an AI's "mental state" could be based on behavioral inferences. By way of analogy, juries assess mental states of human defendants by using common knowledge about what mental states it takes to make a person behave in a particular way. Imagine that a robot repeatedly strikes a bystander. The AI's code could be analyzed to determine how it generated the observed behavior and whether that could be analogized to an intent to cause offensive contact. More simply, a jury could infer the robot intended to commit a battery if it pursued the bystander after she attempted to flee and it continued to strike her.

The prevailing theory has it that one is criminally culpable for an action to the extent that it manifests insufficient regard, a form of ill will or indifference that produces mistakes in the way one recognizes, weighs, and responds to the applicable legal reasons for action, for legally protected interests or values. Criminal law does not demand that citizens be motivated by respect for others, or even respect for the law; all it demands is that they do not put their disrespect on display by acting in ways that are inconsistent with attaching proper weight to protected interests and values. Thus, criminal culpability can be seen as being more about what their behavior manifests and less about the nuances of their private motivations, thoughts, and feelings. Simply, as long as one crosses the line and has no affirmative defense, the law may treat the presumption that one's illegal action manifests insufficient regard as being legally conclusive.

By way of analogy, this notion of culpability can account for corporate culpability. If only the legal notion of criminal culpability is required for punishment, then eligibility for punishment requires being capable of behaving in ways that manifest insufficient regard for the legally recognized reasons. Likewise, all that avoiding legal culpability requires is to abstain from actions that are reasonably interpreted as disrespectful forms of conduct stemming from a legally deficient appreciation of the legal reasons. This provides a recipe for how to regard corporations as being criminally culpable in their own right. They possess information-gathering, reasoning, and decision-making procedures by virtue of the hierarchy of employees they are composed of.

Through their members, corporations can engage in conduct that puts on display their insufficient regard for the legally recognized interests of others. For example, if a corporation learns, through its employees, that its manufacturing processes generate dangerous waste that is seeping into the drinking water in a nearby town, this is a legally recognized reason for altering its conduct. If the corporation resumes its activities unchanged, this demonstrates that it – through its information-sharing and decision-making procedures – does not end up attaching sufficient weight to the legally recognized reasons against continuing its dangerous manufacturing activities. This is paradigmatic criminal culpability.

AI could qualify as criminally culpable in an analogous manner. Sophisticated AI may have built-in goals with a greater or lesser autonomy to determine the means of completing those goals. AI may gather information, process it, and determine the most efficient means to accomplishing them. Accordingly, the law may deem some AI to possess the functional equivalent of sufficient reasoning and decision-making abilities to manifest insufficient regard. For instance, if the AI is programmed to be able to take account of the interests of humans and consider legal requirements but ends up behaving in a way that is inconsistent with taking proper account of these legally recognized interests and reasons.

To determine when sophisticated AI could be said to possess a functional analogue of a standard mens rea, work in philosophy of action characterizing the functional roles of an intention in a person could be extended to AI. In philosopher Michael Bratman's account, actors who intend (i.e., act with the purpose) to bring about an outcome "guide [their] conduct in the direction of causing" that outcome.[15] This means that "in the normal case, one [who intends an outcome] is prepared to make adjustments in what one is doing in response to indications of one's success or failure in promoting" that outcome.[16] So, if the actor is driving with the intention to hit a pedestrian, and should the actor detect that conditions have changed so as to require behavioral adjustments to make this outcome more likely, then an actor with this intention will be disposed to make these adjustments.

This conception of intention could be applied to AI. If an AI is monitoring conditions around it to identify ways to make the outcome (harm a bystander) more likely, and it is then disposed to make behavioral adjustments to make the outcome more likely relative to its background probability of occurring, either as a goal in itself or as a means to accomplishing another goal, the AI could be said to have the purpose of causing that outcome.

Similar strategies could be developed for arguing that an AI possessed other mens rea. For example, knowledge could be attributed to an actor when the actor has a sufficiently robust set of dispositions pertaining to the truth of a proposition, such as the disposition to assent to the proposition if queried, to express surprise and update one's plans if the proposition is revealed to be false, to behave consistently with the truth of the proposition, or to depend on its carrying out one's plans.

In criminal law, knowledge is defined as practical certainty. Thus, if the dispositional theory is extended to AI, there is an argument for saying an AI knows a fact, F, if the AI displays a sufficiently robust set of dispositions associated with the truth of F, such as the disposition to respond affirmatively if queried whether F is practically certain to be true, the disposition to revise plans upon receiving information showing that F is not practically certain, or the disposition to behave as if F is practically certain to be true. If enough of these dispositions are proven, then the knowledge that F is known could be attributed to the AI. One could take a similar approach to arguing that recklessness is present as well, as this requires only awareness that a substantial risk of harm is present (i.e., knowledge that the risk has a mid-level probability of materializing).

True Punishment

A final Eligibility Challenge to AI punishment is that AI cannot be truly "punished." Punishment and criminal conviction are used synonymously in this chapter, but under Hart's definition, punishment "must involve pain or other consequences normally considered unpleasant."[7] Even if an AI is convicted of an offense and subject to negative treatment, such as being reprogrammed or terminated, this may not be punishment because AI cannot experience things as painful or unpleasant.

One response to this objection is to argue that AI punishment does satisfy Hart's definition of punishment, which only requires the treatment in question be normally considered unpleasant – not that it actually be unpleasant. This allows Hart's definition to accommodate people who, for idiosyncratic reasons, do not experience their sentence as unpleasant. The mere fact that a convicted party overtly wants to be imprisoned, like the Norwegian mass murder Anders Bering Breivik who sought conviction and imprisonment to further his political agenda, does not mean that doing so pursuant to a conviction ceases to be punishment. Something similar can be said for defendants who, perhaps like AI, are physically or psychologically incapable of experiencing pain or distress.

Why might punishment need to be normally regarded as unpleasant? Why does it still seem to be punishment, for example, to imprison a person who in no way experiences it as unwelcome? The answer may be that defendants can have interests that are objectively set back, even when they do not subjectively experience these setbacks negatively. Some philosophers argue that it is intrinsically bad for humans to have their physical or agential capacities diminished, regardless of whether this is perceived as harmful.[18] If correct, this suggests that Hart's definition requires punishment to involve events that objectively hinder interests, and that negative subjective experiences are merely one way to objectively set back interests.

Can AI have objective interests? Some philosophers argue that things like nutrition, reproduction, or physical damage are good or bad for biological entities like plants or animals.[19] This is in virtue of something's having identifiable functions that things can be good or bad for it. Most notably, Philippa Foot defends this sort of view (tracing it to Aristotle) when she argues that the members of a given species can be evaluated as excellent or defective by reference to the functions that are built into its characteristic form of life. If having interests in this sense is all that is required for punishment to be sensible, then perhaps AI fits the bill. AI has a range of functions – characteristic patterns of behavior needed to continue in good working order and to succeed at the tasks it characteristically undertakes. If living organisms can, in a thin sense, be said to have an interest in survival and reproduction, ultimately in virtue of their biological programming, then arguably an AI following digital programming could have interests in this sense as well.

Other philosophers reject this view and insist that only entities capable of having beliefs and desires, or at least phenomenal experiences such as pleasure and pain, can truly be said to have interests that are normatively important. Legal philosopher Joel Feinberg takes the capacity for cognition as the touchstone full-blooded interests, that is, as a precondition for having things be good or bad for people. Although "Aristotle and Aquinas took trees [and plants] to have their own 'natural ends,'" Feinberg denies plants "the status of beings with interests of their own" because "an interest, however the concept is finally to be analyzed, presupposes at least rudimentary cognitive equipment."[20] Interests, he says, "are compounded out of *desires* and *aims*, both of which presuppose something like *belief*, or cognitive awareness." In this view, since AI is not capable of cognitive awareness, it cannot possess full-blooded interests of the kind Feinberg has in mind.

A stronger type of reply to the punishment objection is to distinguish between conviction and punishment, where the latter covers the sentence to which the convicted party is subject. Even if no form of treatment can count as punishment unless the entity in question experiences it negatively, this is not a precondition for a conviction. Perhaps for it to be intelligible to convict X of an offense, it is only required that X act in ways that violate a prohibition, and this can be sensibly construed as a manifestation of insufficient regard. If so, then while punishing AI may not be conceptually possible, applying criminal law to AI so that it can be convicted of offenses is. Society could still benefit from AI convictions while not running afoul of the conceptual confusion in purporting to punish AI. And even if applying criminal law to AI is conceptually confusing, it could still have good consequences to call it punishment when AI is convicted. This would be not to defend AI punishment from within existing criminal law principles but to suggest that there are consequentialist reasons to depart from them.

Additional Challenges and Considerations

Reducibility

One could object that there is never a genuine need to punish AI because any time an AI seems criminally culpable in its own right, this culpability can always be reduced to that of nearby human actors, such as developers, owners, and users, whom the law could target. This concern has been raised against corporate punishment, too. Skeptics argue that corporate culpability is always fully reducible to culpable actions of individual humans. Any time a corporation does something intuitively culpable – like causing a harmful oil spill through insufficient safety procedures – this can always be fully reduced to the culpability of the individuals involved: the person who carried out the safety checks, the designers who devised the safety protocols, the managers who pushed employees to cut corners in search of savings, etc. For any case offered to demonstrate the irreducibility of corporate culpability, a skeptic may use creative means to find additional wrongdoing by other individual actors further afield or in the past to account for the apparent corporate culpability.

This worry may not be as acute for AI as it is for corporations. AI seems able to behave in ways that are more autonomous (and less predictable and foreseeable) from its developers than corporations are from their members. In any case, there are ways to block the reducibility worry for corporate as well as for AI culpability. The simplest response is to recall that legal culpability is the concern, not moral blameworthiness. Specifically, it would be bad policy for criminal law, in all cases, to allow any putative corporate criminal culpability to always be fully reduced to individual criminal liability.

To ensure that corporate criminal culpability can in every case be reduced to individual criminal culpability would require criminalizing minute acts of individual misconduct – momentary lapses of attention, the failure to perceive emerging problems that are difficult to notice, tiny bits of carelessness, mistakes in prioritizing time and resources, not being sufficiently critical of groupthink, and so on. Mature legal systems should not criminalize infinitely fine-grained forms of misconduct, as doing so would be invasive and threaten values like autonomy and freedom of expression and association, but rather they should focus on broader and more serious categories of directly harmful misconduct that can be straightforwardly defined, identified, and prosecuted.

Instead, culpability deficits should exist in any well-designed system of criminal law, and this in turn creates a genuine need for corporate criminal culpability as an irreducible concept. Similarly, there is reason to think it would be a bad system to encourage law enforcement and prosecutors, any time an AI causes harm, to invasively delve into the internal activities of the organizations' developing the AI in search of minute individual misconduct – perhaps even the slightest negligence or failure to plan for highly unlikely exigencies. Hence, where AI is concerned, the reducibility challenge – at least as applied to legal culpability – does not impose a categorical bar to punishing AI.

Spillover

The corporate context illustrates another objection to AI punishment: spillover. Because corporate punishments – usually in the form of fines – amount to a hit to a corporation's bottom line, these punishments inevitably spill over onto innocent shareholders. This may seem to violate the desert constraint against the state harming people in excess of their desert, and the same objection has been raised against punishing AI. Christina Mulligan worries that

> one could ... imagine situations where the notion of separating a rogue robot from its owner [or damaging or restricting the robot in punishing it] would create a disproportionate burden on the owner, for example if a robot was unique, unusually expensive relative to the harm caused, or difficult to replace.[21]

If an AI unforeseeably causes harm, it could seem unfair or disproportionate to its owners or operators to damage the AI in punishment.

There are familiar responses to the spillover objection for corporations. One could contend that spillover does not qualify as punishment because it is not imposed on a shareholder for her offense. Nonetheless, this definitional answer is somewhat unsatisfying, as there clearly are strong reasons for the state not to knowingly harm innocent bystanders, even if it does not strictly count as punishment. A better answer is that spillover is not a special problem for corporate or AI punishment. Most forms of punishment – including punishment of individual wrongdoers – have the potential to harm the innocent, as when a convicted person has dependent children. Spillover objections may simply expose general problems with criminal law. The fact that punishment tends to harm the innocent suggests a need to reform criminal law as well as prisons, reentry programs, and similar initiatives to lessen the collateral consequences of punishment of all types.

In the corporate context, some have recently responded to the spillover objection by defending reforms to corporate punishments, so the "pain" they impose is more directly distributed to the culpable actors within the company who contributed to the crime. When it comes to punishing AI, similar thinking applies. AI punishment should be narrowly tailored. Destroying an AI, for example, would be a blunt remedy that is more likely to harm the innocent. More custom remedies could be implemented instead, such as reprogramming the AI or directing fines at responsible persons. In such ways, the punishment of AI systems could be crafted to minimize the spillover effects. Further, spillover may be less of a concern in the case of AI-generated crime, where there may be little nexus between AI punishment and harm to innocent individuals. Spillover thus is not an absolute bar to AI punishment. It is an omnipresent problem with criminal punishment, which must be addressed whether for corporations or AI.

Other Costs

Punishing AI entails serious practical challenges and substantial changes to criminal law. For instance, there might be enforcement problems with punishing distributed AI on a blockchain. Such AI may be particularly difficult to effectively combat or deactivate. Even if the practical issues are resolved, punishing AI would still require major changes to criminal law. Legal personality may be necessary to charge and convict an AI of a crime, and conferring legal personhood on AI would create a whole new mode of criminal liability, much the way that corporate criminal liability constitutes one beyond individual criminal liability.

Over the years, there have been many proposals for extending some kind of legal personality to AI. Most famously, a 2017 report by the European Parliament called on the European Commission to create a legislative instrument to deal with "civil liability caused by robots."[22] It further requested that the commission consider "a specific legal status for robots" or "possibly [apply] electronic personality" as one solution to tort liability. Even in such a speculative and tentative form, this proposal proved highly controversial. More than 150 AI "experts" subsequently sent an open letter to the European Commission warning that "from an ethical and legal perspective, creating a legal personality for a robot is inappropriate whatever the legal status model."[23]

Full-fledged legal personality for AI equivalent to that afforded to natural persons, with all the legal rights that they enjoy, would clearly be inappropriate. For example, allowing AI to vote would undermine democracy, given the ease with which anyone looking to determine the outcome of an election could create AI systems to vote for a designated candidate. However, the rights and obligations associated with legal personality vary, even for natural persons such as children who are treated differently than adults.

Crucially, no artificial person enjoys all the same rights and obligations as a natural person. Companies – the best-known class of artificial persons – have long enjoyed only a limited set of rights and obligations that allows them to sue and be sued, enter contracts, incur debt, own property, and be convicted of crimes. However, they do not receive protection under constitutional provisions such as the Equal Protection Clause of the Fourteenth Amendment, nor can they bear arms, run for or hold public office, marry, or enjoy other fundamental rights possessed by natural persons. Thus, granting legal personality to AI in order to allow its punishment would not require AI to receive the rights afforded to natural persons, or even those afforded to companies. AI legal personality could consist solely of obligations.

Even so, any sort of legal personhood for AI would be a dramatic legal change that could prove problematic. Providing legal personality to AI could result in increased anthropomorphisms. People who humanize AI expect it to adhere to social norms and have higher expectations of its capabilities. This is problematic where such expectations are inaccurate and AI is operating from a position of trust. Such anthropomorphisms could result in "cognitive and psychological damages to manipulability and reduced quality of life"[24] for users. These outcomes may be more likely if AI were held accountable by the state in ways normally reserved only for human members of society. Strengthening questionable anthropomorphic tendencies regarding AI could also lead to more violent or destructive behavior directed at AI, such as vandalism. In addition, punishing AI could also affect human well-being in less direct ways, such as by producing anxiety about one's own status within society due to the perception that AI is given a legal status on par with human beings.

The appeal to expressive benefits to justify the punishment of AI is also worrisome. Punishing AI to placate those who want retaliation for AI-generated harms would be akin to giving in to mob justice. If society legitimizes such reactions, it might enable populist calls for justice to be pressed more forcefully in the future. The mere fact that punishing AI might be popular would not show the practice to be just. David Lewis observes that if it is unjust for the population to "demand blood" in response to seeing harm, then it would be equally unjust to satisfy such demands through the law – even if "it might be prudent to ignore justice and do their bidding."[25] Moreover, punishing AI for expressivist purposes could lead to further bad behavior on the part of the state, which could spill over to the way humans are treated. Kate Darling has argued that robots should be protected from cruelty in order to reflect moral norms and prevent undesirable human behavior.[26]

Finally, conferring legal personality on AI could lead to rights creep. Even if AI is given few or no rights when initially granted legal personhood, AI may gradually acquire rights over time. In a 1933 Supreme Court opinion, Justice Louis Brandeis warned about rights creep, arguing that giving companies an excess of rights could allow them to dominate the state. Eighty years after that decision, Justice Brandeis' concerns were prescient in light of Supreme Court jurisprudence in cases such as *Citizen's United* and *Hobby Lobby*, which significantly expanded the rights extended to corporations.[27]

Insights to Human Punishment

Thinking about AI punishment helps to provide fresh understanding into criminal law theory with respect to justifying how people are punished. For instance, some philosophers argue that people who engage in antisocial behavior are not morally blameworthy, and therefore that punishment cannot be justified on the basis of culpability. The theory of determinism holds that people can only ever make a single set of choices. If people were able to identically re-create the exact conditions of their lives – from their genetics to birth environment to the opportunities that they encounter – they would make the same choices. Some proponents of this theory further believe it means that free will does not exist. If correct, it calls into question the role of culpability in criminal law.

Without free will, people cannot be morally blameworthy for their bad behavior. If AI can sensibly be punished, it helps to answer this concern because it would suggest that moral fault is less important than previously thought, and imply that criminal law is more concerned about behavior that manifests a lack of respect for protected values than whether someone is deep down a bad person. AI punishment pushes back against claims that punishments are not justified because people lack free will.

As a practical matter, reasoning about AI punishment indicates that the law should do less to criminalize motives than antisocial behavior. It undermines support for so-called thought crimes, such as the United Kingdom's Terrorism Act of 2006, which criminalizes "engaging in any conduct in preparation for giving effect to [a terroristic] intention."[28] In effect, this makes just about any activity illegal if someone has the requisite mental state.

4 FEASIBLE ALTERNATIVES

There are potential costs and benefits to AI punishment, as well as challenges to doctrinal commitments of the law. At this point, to determine whether AI punishment is desirable requires investigating whether there are better responses to AI-generated crime.

First Alternative: The Status Quo

The first alternative is the simplest – do nothing. If only a single AI-generated crime is committed each decade, there would be far less need to change the law than if AI-generated crime were a daily occurrence. The absence of evidence suggesting that AI-generated crime is common counsels against taking potentially costly actions now, but this balance could change as technological advances result in more AI activity. Still, the current risk of AI's committing criminal sorts of harms without accountability does argue in favor of some sort of legal response – even if nothing as radical as AI punishment.

Creative interpretations of current laws may provide at least a partial response to AI-generated crimes. As Hallevy observes, cases of this sort could possibly be prosecuted under an innocent "agency model," assuming AI can sensibly be treated as meeting the preconditions of an innocent agent, even if not a fully criminally responsible agent in its own right. Under the innocent agency doctrine, criminal liability can attach to a person who acts through an agent who lacks capacity, such as a child. For instance, if an adult uses a five-year-old to deliver illegal drugs, the adult rather than the child would generally be criminally liable. Innocent agency could be analogous to a person's programming a sophisticated AI to break the law: The person has liability for intentionally causing the AI to bring about the external elements of the offense. This doctrine requires intent – or at least the knowledge – that the innocent agent will cause the prohibited result in question. This means that the innocent agency model does not provide a route to liability in cases where someone does not intend or foresee that the AI system's being used will cause harm. Finally, innocent or otherwise, an agent must commit a criminal act and so this still runs up against the Eligibility Challenge.

Second Alternative: Conventionally Extending Criminal Law

The problem of AI-generated crime would be more reasonably addressed through more traditional extensions of criminal law, including the creation of crimes for individuals. An "AI Abuse Act" could punish those persons for malicious or reckless uses of AI, just as the Computer Fraud and Abuse Act criminalizes gaining unauthorized access to information using personal computers. Such an act could also penalize the failure to responsibly design, deploy, test, train, and monitor the AI that a person contributed to developing. New negligence crimes could also be added for developers who design systems that foreseeably could produce a risk of any serious harm or unlawful consequence, even if a specific risk is unforeseeable.

Yet, extending criminal law in this manner might unreasonably stifle innovation and commercial activities. Moreover, some of these activities do not seem to amount to individually culpable conduct, as all activities and technologies involve some risk of harm. If developing a system that could produce any unlawful consequence were a crime, all the early developers of the Internet would likely be guilty of it. As a final shortfall, these new crimes would target individual conduct culpable along familiar dimensions and have limited utility with regard to AI-generated crimes that do not reduce to culpable actors. Accordingly, a different way to expand criminal law seems needed to address AI-generated crime.

More ambitiously, in cases of AI-generated crime, a designated adjacent person could be punished who would not otherwise be directly criminally liable – a "responsible person." This could involve new forms of criminal negligence for failing to discharge statutory duties in order to make a person liable in cases of AI-generated crime. It could be a requirement for anyone who is creating or operating an AI capable of causing harm to ex ante register a responsible person for the AI and a crime not to designate a responsible person. This would be akin to the offense of driving without a license. The registration system could be maintained by a federal agency. However, a registration scheme is problematic because it is difficult to distinguish between AI capable of and AI not capable of criminal activity, especially when dealing with unforeseeable criminal activity. Even simple and innocuous-seeming AI could end up causing serious harm. Registration may also involve a substantial administrative burden, and the costs associated with mandatory registration may outweigh any benefits given AI's increasing prevalence.

A default rule rather than a registration system may be preferable. The responsible person could be the AI's manufacturer or supplier if it is a commercial product. If it is not, the responsible person could be the AI's owner, developer if no owner exists, or user if no developer can be identified. Even noncommercial AI is usually owned as property, although this may not always be the case, for instance, with some open-source software. Similarly, all AI has human developers, and in the event an AI ever autonomously creates another AI, responsibility for the criminal acts of an AI-created AI could reach back to the original AI's owner.

In the event an AI's developer cannot be identified, or potentially if there are a large number of developers, again in the case of some open-source software, responsibility could attach to an AI's user. However, this would fail to catch the rare (perhaps only hypothetical) case of the noncommercial AI with no owner, no identifiable developer, and no user. To the extent that a noncommercial AI owner, developer, and user who are working together would prefer a different responsibility arrangement, they could be permitted to agree to a different ex ante selection of the responsible person. This may be more likely to occur with sophisticated parties where there is a greater risk of AI-generated crime. The responsible person could even be an artificial person such as a corporation.

It would be possible to impose criminal liability on a responsible person directly in the event of AI-generated crime. If new statutory duties of supervision and care are defined regarding the AI for which the responsible person is answerable, then criminal negligence liability could be imposed should she unreasonably fail to discharge those duties. Granted, this would not be punishment for the harmful conduct of the AI itself. Rather, it would be a form of direct criminal liability imposed on the responsible person for her own conduct.

If this does not go far enough to address AI-generated crime, criminal liability could also be imposed on the responsible person on a strict liability basis, particularly if the relevant punishments are only fines rather than incarceration. Strict liability crimes are generally restricted to minor infractions or regulatory offenses or "violations," though examples of more serious strict criminal liability can also be found, such as statutory rape in some jurisdictions. Yet, there are serious problems with strict liability crimes applied to persons. If justifiable at all, they can only be used as a last resort in exigent circumstances – as in cases of unusually dangerous activities.

However, it is not obvious that the use of AI qualifies as unusually dangerous. To the contrary, in many areas of activity it would be unreasonable not to use AI, as when safety can be improved over human actors such as will be the case with self-driving cars. Most bad human actors who use AI systems to commit crimes will still be caught under existing criminal laws, and so far there have not been any high-profile cases of AI-generated crime. As a result, AI-generated crime is not yet a significant enough social problem to merit the use of strict criminal liability.

Ultimately, a responsible person regime accompanied by new statutory duties, which carry criminal penalties if these duties are negligently or recklessly breached, provides a potential approach to dealing with AI-generated crime. Expressing condemnation through a criminal conviction of the responsible person can achieve much of the expressive benefit from a direct conviction of AI – and without as serious a loss of public trust as the legal fictions needed to punish AI directly would create.

Third Alternative: Expanded Civil Liability

Civil law, primarily tort law, could be a method of both imposing legal account-ability and deterring harmful AI. Some AI crime will no doubt already result in civil liability, but it comes with built-in limitations. Very few laws specifically address AI-generated harms, which means civil liability must typically be established under a traditional negligence or product liability framework or under contractual liability. Negligence generally requires a person to act carelessly, so there may be no recovery where this cannot be established in cases of AI-generated crime. Product liability may require that both an AI be a commercial product (e.g., this may not apply where AI is used as a "service") and there be a defect in the product (or that its properties be falsely represented). In the case of complex AI, it may be difficult to prove a defect, and AI may cause harm without a "defect" in the product liability sense. Civil liability may also derive from contractual relationships, but this usually only applies where there is a contract between parties. This, too, may also have significant limitations.

To the extent there is inadequate civil liability for AI-generated crime, the responsible person proposal sketched previously could be repurposed so that the responsible person could only be civilly liable. The case against a responsible person could be akin to a tort action if brought by an individual or a class of plaintiffs, or a civil enforcement action if brought by a government agency tasked with regulating AI. At trial, an AI would not be treated like a corporation, where the corporation itself is held to have done the harmful act and the law treats it as a singular acting and "thinking" entity. Rather, the question for adjudication would be whether the responsible person discharged his duties of care in respect of the AI in a reasonable way – or else civil liability could also be imposed on a strict liability basis.

A responsible person scheme is not the only solution to inadequate civil liability for AI-generated crime. An insurance scheme is another approach. Owners, devel-opers, or users of AI, or just certain types of AI, could pay a tax into a fund to ensure adequate compensation for victims of AI-generated crime. The cost of this tax would be relatively minor compared to the financial value generated by AI. An AI com-pensation fund could operate like the National Vaccine Injury Compensation Program (VICP), which is funded by a tax on vaccines that users pay. Vaccines result in widespread social benefit but are known in rare cases to cause serious problems. VICP is a no-fault alternative to traditional tort liability that compensates individuals injured by a VICP-covered vaccine. In the event that someone is harmed as a result of AI-generated crime, he would then have recourse to compensation from the fund.

Further Thoughts

At least for now, punishing AI would be an overreaction to all but largely hypothetical concerns. Alternative approaches could provide substantially similar benefits and avoid many of the problems with AI punishment. Civil liability is a more appropriate response given the scope of the problem and the risk of chilling socially valuable activities. Modest expansions to criminal law would still be preferable to AI punishment, such as new negligence crimes centered around the improper design, operation, and testing of AI applications, as well as possible criminal penalties for designated parties who fail to discharge statutory duties, in the event that AI-generated crimes become a more significant social problem.

Yet, as with the idea of AI's paying taxes, criminally punishing AI is not as absurd an idea as it may initially seem. Criminal law can – and, where corporations are involved, already does – appeal to elaborate legal fictions to provide a pragmatic tool for solving social problems. Nonetheless, legal fictions must be used with caution, as their overuse risks eroding public trust and weakening the rule of law. Moreover, allowing legal fictions to proliferate unchecked can lead to widespread injustice through punishing either the innocent or more harshly than one's culpability calls for. For this reason, there is and should be an onerous burden to meet before we can be confident that a particular legal fiction – such as legal personality for AI or the invention of culpable mental states for AI – is adopted.

7

Alternative Perspectives on AI Legal Neutrality

We can only see a short distance ahead, but we can see plenty there that needs to be done.

– Alan Turing

The preceding chapters have considered in detail how the law distinguishes, often inadvertently, between behavior by people and AI and how this has unintended consequences. The present tax laws disadvantage human workers, and if not addressed this may reduce the government's revenue. In torts, the different standards applied to AI and people could worsen safety once AI becomes a safer and more efficient actor for certain tasks such as driving. Intellectual property law may fail to encourage innovation in a world where AI is creating and inventing. And, criminal law does not have appropriate responses for AI's causing criminal sorts of harms. This book has argued in all of these areas that application of AI legal neutrality will help the law better achieve its underlying goals – whether promoting competition, improving safety, incentivizing innovation, or reducing antisocial behavior.

This chapter considers some further implications and criticisms of AI legal neutrality. First, AI legal neutrality is a valuable principle, regardless of whether AI broadly achieves superhuman performance, and the law would not want to deliberately disadvantage AI to limit competition. Second, this principle can be coherently applied to different legal areas, even though it does not demand legally identical treatment of people and AI and even though it may be at odds with other best principles of AI regulation such as preserving human agency. Finally, this chapter considers some of the unique risks and challenges posed by AI and argues that these are not as novel or unmanageable as sometimes claimed.

1 AI LEGAL NEUTRALITY AND THE SINGULARITY

Some of the arguments in this book give credibility to the predictions of technologists who believe the singularity will occur in our lifetimes. However, other prognosticators think AI's potential has been vastly overstated, that the current round of predictions is mostly hype. What if automation does not increase unemployment rates, self-driving cars never significantly exceed the performance of human drivers, and AI inventors remain a permanent novelty? The singularity may never come; and if it does, it may not come this century. Is there value in a principle of AI legal neutrality without superintelligent AI?

Paradoxically, AI legal neutrality becomes more important in a world where AI does not dramatically outperform people. Laws that result in unequal treatment of AI will be most disruptive when people and AI are in relatively close competition. Ultimately, if AI becomes not just more but substantially more efficient than people, then differential legal treatment will only delay automation. Today, the decision by McDonald's to replace (or not) a person with a mediocre-performing $35,000 robotic arm is influenced by tax policy. However, a less expensive robot, costing about $3,500, that is both faster and more accurate than a person will prompt McDonald's to automate regardless of the taxes levied on AI. AI legal neutrality might simply accelerate the adoption of automation when it is more efficient.

The principle of AI legal neutrality encourages automation when it is more efficient, and according to technological optimists, AI will eventually be more efficient at essentially everything. The picture this paints for some is that people will eventually live in a world where AI does everything and people do very little – a dystopian nightmare, if you will, in which people lose the opportunity for work and a sense of meaning and purpose. The question becomes this: Should the law disadvantage AI to prevent this outcome? Discriminatory laws will not stop automation, unless absolute prohibitions on using AI for certain activities, such as banning its use in any commercial diagnosis or treatment of disease, are adopted.

If complete injunctions on particular activities were implemented, this could ensure the supremacy of human decision-making in medicine and prevent the displacement of doctors, but broadly prohibiting AI activity would be undesirable. In health care, the result for patients would be inferior medical care at higher prices. The situation would be no more desirable for doctors. If they were inclined to find meaning through productivity, they would not find it here as their efforts would be entirely pointless. In this future, doctors would be employed to prevent a vastly superior AI from doing their job better – not to help others. In essence, this would be a reenactment of the fable of Sisyphus, the cruel Greek king condemned for all eternity by the gods to push a large boulder to the top of a steep hill only to see it roll down as he nears the hill's peak. The solution to managing the challenge of automation should not be a curse of endless, pointless (if not harmful) labor.

In this (nearly) fully automated future, there might be limited circumstances, such as making decisions to use deadly force or criminally punish a defendant, when automation would be inappropriate. However, the world can only accommodate so many judges and police officers if certain professions such as these are reserved for people. At some point, this would mean that the majority of people will need to find ways to occupy their time with activities other than work. Thomas More writes in *Utopia* about an idealized communal society where people rise early, work six hours a day, and spend the rest of the day on their own with the caveat that they spend it wisely. In an AI utopia, there might not be a need for people to work six hours a day – or at all. While people find meaning in many things, they will not likely find it through simple productivity in this future.

Plato believed that the meaning of life comes from attaining knowledge. Perhaps, with a virtually unlimited amount of leisure time and resources, people will choose to engage in continuous self-improvement. Confucianists see meaning in human relationships, as Tu Weiming wrote, "[W]e can realize the ultimate meaning of life in ordinary human existence."[1] Perhaps, people will spend their time cultivating personal connections. Jeremy Bentham thought the meaning is to bring the greatest happiness to the greatest number of people – the greatest happiness principle. Perhaps, people will spend their days enjoying virtual reality.

While it is beyond the scope of this book to establish the meaning of life, it is sufficient to note that there are paths to meaning other than through work. Also, it may be paternalistic to dictate to others what it means to spend one's time wisely, and certainly it is to force them to labor for their "own" benefit. This is not to say that the singularity is guaranteed to improve well-being, but a realistic dystopian AI future is unlikely to be killer robots run amok or a life without meaning. Our concerns should be about a future where AI only benefits a small number of individuals, particularly if this occurs at the expense of the less fortunate. The way to prevent that future is not by prohibiting automation but by having the appropriate legal frameworks.

2 AI LEGAL NEUTRALITY'S COHERENCE

This book has argued that legally identical treatment of people and AI would be undesirable, even as legal regimes tend to function better when they do not discriminate between AI and human behavior. AI legal neutrality does not require direct criminal punishment of AI, AI liability for accidents, or AI ownership of intellectual property. One might therefore object that acceptance of the principle of AI legal neutrality would be impractical, even unworkable, for policymakers who favor consistency in application. This concern also applies to other AI principles.

In 2019, the European Commission's High-Level Expert Group on AI put forward guidelines of seven key requirements or principles that AI systems should meet, including transparency, privacy, human agency, and nondiscrimination.[2] It is hard to object to any of these in the abstract. In practice, however, these requirements might conflict with each other. For instance, transparency might come at the expense of privacy. Understanding how a connectionist AI functions could require access to its training inputs, which often consist of personal data. Making them available for inspection could violate a right to privacy, a particularly acute violation with an AI's being applied in health care, for instance. Transparency might also require the disclosure of commercially valuable confidential information. Access to an AI's code might be necessary to understand its function, but if competitors can access this code, they might be able to create similar products without violating intellectual property protections.

Similarly, human agency might conflict with nondiscrimination. Discrimination by algorithms, or algorithmic bias, is a long-standing concern, also one that more prominently entered the public consciousness as a result of reporting in 2016 by ProPublica about a proprietary sentencing algorithm, Correctional Offender Management Profiling for Alternative Sanctions (COMPAS), that ProPublica claims systematically discriminated against black defendants. COMPAS helps judges make bail determinations (whether to release or secure people in advance of their trial) by providing risk assessments of defendants. The algorithm more often labeled black defendants who subsequently did not reoffend as high risk and white defendants who did as low risk.[3] The company argued in response that there was a roughly equal proportion of white and black defendants at any specific risk level.

The broader concern of biased algorithms remains, regardless of whether one specific AI makes racially biased determinations. Biases are an inevitable part of both AI and human decision-making, but some are morally and legally unacceptable. Biased algorithms are not the result of a person deliberately engineering AI to be, say, racist but they might arise if, for example, connectionist AI learns based on biased training data. If human judges have historically sentenced defendants in a discriminatory fashion, AI might do so in the future.

While the incorporation of historical biases is a legitimate concern about AI, it ignores another problematic implication of algorithmic bias, which is that human judges have discriminated against minority defendants – consciously or unconsciously – despite such discrimination's being legally prohibited. It can be very difficult to detect, much less alter, human biases. In 2019, for instance, France made publishing data analysis related to judicial decisions a crime punishable by five years' imprisonment.[4] The French government makes judicial decisions together with the names of judges publicly available, but it is illegal to aggregate data and create a record of a specific judge. A critic of this law would assume it is an attempt to prevent demonstration of inconsistency and bias in judgments. Existing studies have discovered "amazing disparities" in the outcomes of cases based on how a judge decides a case.[5]

Human decision-making may not only lack transparency but also have poorer explainability than AI's. True, a judge, unlike some AI, can be relied upon to explain a decision. However, the explanation is not guaranteed to be accurate. A judge who is consciously biased against a protected group is unlikely to admit to such a bias. Instead, he will rationalize an explanation for a sentence by relying on the facts of the offense, a defendant's personal circumstances, and other factors. And, if a judge has an unconscious bias, then he is not even aware of this distortion in perspective.

The human mind is, perhaps, more algorithmic black box than AI. When properly queried, AI is more transparent about its internal rules, which can also be explicitly overwritten. However, no amount of training is guaranteed to internalize rules in people. For instance, the law has told human judges that it is illegal to discriminate on the basis of race, yet some of them have still issued racially biased judgments. A way to manage human bias is to cede some agency to AI, which can be explicitly programmed to never consider race or even proxy variables; doing so might be the best chance for society to avoid discrimination in a racially stratified world.

While transparency, privacy, human agency, and nondiscrimination are important principles, they are conceptual guideposts rather than absolute prescriptions. Intelligent policymaking requires that a decision maker consider how to balance these concepts on a case-by-case basis. Different jurisdictions also have distinct cultural and value preferences. For instance, some countries are more concerned with user privacy than others, and there are others that highly value entrepreneurship and give greater rights in user data to private companies.

Protecting Spheres of Human Agency

A frequently invoked principle of AI regulation is maintaining the supremacy of human agency that may be at odds with the principle of AI legal neutrality. Should automation be excluded from some areas of human activity, such as creative work, even when it is more efficient? Harlan Howard famously described country music as "three chords and the truth."[6] This statement may not be entirely accurate in its description of country music from a technical standpoint, but it is certainly true that there are a finite number of tones that human ears can distinguish as well as a finite number of ways to combine these tones.

Already, there are more human-composed songs than a person could listen to, even if the they were played one after the other, every day, for the entirety of that person's life. When every possible five-minute basic audio recording is calculated, which would include things not typically thought of as music, the result is an incomprehensible number: something like $2\char`^211,000,000$.[7] The number is significantly smaller when the recordings are limited to tones people can distinguish, such as typical melodies. The number becomes smaller still if an AI is only concerned with creating music people are likely to enjoy. Still, by any measure, it remains a mind-bogglingly large number that only a futuristic AI with vastly expanded capabilities could possibly generate.

There may be limited value in generating every conceivable five-minute recording, given the practical impossibility of a person's listening to all that content, unless an AI could also evaluate its output for usefulness. An AI could hypothetically determine which recordings are most likely to be enjoyable to people, or perhaps even to specific people.[8] This AI could then provide each person with their optimal musical playlist, rank ordered, with the songs they are most likely to enjoy every day for the rest of their lives. If such a system could be created, should it? There is a benefit to AI's creating new music that people will enjoy, but will this ability by AI have a chilling effect on human creativity and the lives of musicians? The same two questions apply to other creative areas. For instance, the human eye can only distinguish pictures up to a certain resolution, which is already being exceeded by some cutting-edge monitors. With a finite number of pixels in a monitor, an AI should hypothetically be able to create every possible image. Will this disincentivize human photographers?

Of course, people will continue to create. People have not stopped playing chess, even though AI's chess supremacy is now unquestioned. Self-improvement and competition against other people are still worthwhile endeavors. Likewise, long-distance running used to have serious practical importance when it was the quickest means of transmitting a message. In fact, the marathon race was inspired by the story of Pheidippides, who died running from Marathon to Athens to announce a military victory. Running long distances lost much of its practical importance with the introduction of faster means of transportation, yet people still run marathons. People value personal improvement, the social aspects of activities, and competition against other people. In fifty years, someone might make music because they enjoy the act of it, or because there is a market specifically for music made by people. In an AI utopia, people would continue to be creative simply because they enjoy doing so.

What about spheres of activity where there is less concern about protectionism and more concern about bad outcomes? AI lacks both common sense and an internal moral compass (although the same thing might be said about some people). Automation seems to give rise to special concern with respect to certain military or judicial activities. Some of the most strenuous objections to automation revolve around "killer robots," or the concept of a lethal autonomous weapons system (LAWS) that can fully automate life and death decisions. There might be some activities that should never be automated.

On the other hand, some arguments against automation may not always endure. Kenneth Anderson and Matthew C. Waxman have argued in favor of LAWS contending that LAWS will protect one's own personnel as well as civilians.[9] AI can respond more quickly than human soldiers and does not respond emotionally (which can restrain or unleash base instincts) or act in self-interest while some human soldiers have historically failed to respect the law of armed conflict. For some military tasks, AI might more humanely handle situations than people would. It is also notable that there are already some highly automated weapons systems, such as Israel's Iron Dome antimissile system, which cannot effectively function without automation since it detects incoming missiles and deploys countermeasures faster than a human soldier possibly could. Of course, the Iron Dome system is strictly defensive.

Even the judiciary has not proven immune to automation. In late 2019, the government of Estonia initiated a program to have a "robot judge" adjudicate small claims cases.[10] This may be the first instance of an AI's outright taking the place of a judge, though it is too early to evaluate the success of the program and parties are still able to appeal any decision to a person. To date, AI has done much more augmentation than automation of judging, and more often it is employed with respect to mediation, a process by which a neutral third party helps parties voluntarily settle a dispute, than to adjudication, a process by which a neutral third party (usually a judge or arbitrator) provides a binding resolution. The earliest AI to augment third parties was, descriptively enough, called Legal Decisionmaking System at the RAND Corporation in 1980. It helped settle product liability cases by determining liability, case value, and fair settlement value. Modern AI that is being operated this way includes a system called BOS, which the Prosecuting Authority in the Netherlands uses to determine punishment severity – much the way that COMPAS is being used in the United States.

It makes sense to automate rather than augment when you have a conflict that may not justify a traditional third party's involvement – perhaps for low-value, high-volume disputes, where the costs of litigation outweigh the amount in dispute. eBay's dispute resolution system is the first major online dispute resolution success. The company uses a questionnaire-based AI expert system that performs the role of mediator, collecting information, identifying preferences, and suggesting resolution options. eBay reports its system manages sixty million disputes a year, 90 percent of which are resolved without human intervention. An eBay human third party gets involved if the AI cannot resolve matters. eBay also reports an 80 percent satisfaction rate. However, this system is not without its critics.

Automating eBay's dispute system was an obvious business choice, particularly given the low value of most disputes. It is hard to image courts absorbing all those cases, given that many courts already have substantial backlogs. Automation was easier because of eBay's detailed knowledge of the transactions in question and the narrow spectrum of disputes: Customers did not receive their items, the item was not as described, and so forth. In an early version of the system, a human mediator resolved disputes using email. Automating that process increased both settlement rates and participants' reported satisfaction. This was attributed to requiring participants to restrict their communications to preset options and using AI to manage the flow of information. AI can be a neutral to fit the fuss, to paraphrase Frank Sander.[11]

Other AI systems similarly replace mediators, such as CyberSettle and SmartSettle, which use double-blind bidding. The essentials of the such systems and how they are used are basically the same: Parties provide an AI with their offers and bottom lines, and if these offers are within range of one another, the AI can split the difference or offer proposals that bridge the gap. This can change the dynamics of a human-led mediation, which often involves extensive advocacy and inquiry, to focus on the exchange of proposals. Some complex models exist, but at their base these systems are for people who are arguing over a dollar figure. CyberSettle says that it has handled more than 200,000 claims with a combined value of more than $1.6 billion, with an average reduction of settlement time of eighty-five percent.

AI can thus provide a convenient, fast, and inexpensive solution to many disputes. But when disputes become more complicated than standard eBay fare, things get more difficult. Mediation can involve ambiguity, social and emotional issues, and interpersonal and cultural differences – all of which may be challenging for machines to resolve by following simple rules. AI also has a difficult time operating with norms and standards. Still, there is enough potential benefit that AI use is expanding and being applied to increasingly diverse sorts of disputes, even divorce cases, which can get both complicated and emotional. Governments are also increasingly using AI for facilitating adjudication. For example, US states use the system Matterhorn to manage outstanding warrants and traffic violations, small claims, and family disputes.

For AI to successfully automate resolving a wider range of disputes, it needs to be not only efficient but also fair – or at least it has to behave fairly. Some critics think that "machine-made justice" is no substitute for existing processes. In this view, there is no substitute for a person's reasoning and decision-making capabilities, not to mention common sense, for any dispute moderately complex or outside narrow domains. Put another way, critics maintain that fairness and justice are exclusively human traits that AI cannot and should not attempt to replicate. On the other hand, people long believed that AI could never be creative, yet modern AI is making music, writing novels, and painting portraits. AI can be creative if it is programmed to be creative, and it can behave fairly if it is programmed to behave fairly. John McCarthy, who coined the term AI, maintained there is nothing a judge knows that could not be told to a computer.

3 UNIQUE RISKS OF AI AND AI LEGAL NEUTRALITY

The AI does not hate you, nor does it love you, but you are made out of atoms which it can use for something else.

– *Eliezer Yudkowsky*

Sometimes, people and AI act in ways that are functionally interchangeable, but they differ in a substantial number of respects. These differences have been highlighted in a body of literature on AI's risks and negative effects. Scholarship has focused on AI's opacity and lack of explainability, design choices that result in bias, negative impacts on personal well-being and social interactions, and how AI has changed power dynamics in concerning ways between users and private companies (e.g., Facebook's knowledge about its users) and between citizens and the state (e.g., profiling and surveillance). There is no guarantee that AI will not be applied objectionably or co-opted by bad actors merely because AI has the potential to be neutral and "transcend politics."

While AI might identify and solve problems that society is unaware of, it might also cause harm in unpredictable ways. Consider Nick Bostrom's Paperclip Maximizer thought experiment, a sort of modern-day version of the *Sorcerer's Apprentice*.[12] If a sufficiently unconstrained and powerful AI is tasked with maximizing paperclip production, it could determine that the best means of achieving this is to destroy competing sources of manufacturing, obtain resources through war, or even eliminate people it decides are likely to interfere with paperclip production. AI might not have humanlike motives; as such, it could act in ways people find arbitrary or unexpected. All these risks seem to counsel against using AI, or at least proceeding cautiously.

These are genuine concerns that should not be minimized. Indeed, managing these risks should be one of the primary goals of a legal regime responsive to AI. That AI and people can act dissimilarly and generate different sorts of harms is all the more reason to have laws that have been explicitly designed with AI in mind. AI legal neutrality should not be equated with a lack of regulation, nor should it be the only principle of AI regulation. Other principles like accountability and beneficence might be more important in some cases.

Also, while there are benefits to nonbinding, voluntary ethical codes to guide conduct, these same principles should be the foundation of compulsory regulatory frameworks where the risks are sufficiently great. Managing risk is not a novel problem for the law, and many of the underlying concerns with AI can be dealt with under existing schemes or with modest changes. The legal frameworks that provide a balance between state authority and individual privacy rights are already in place. Those frameworks might need to be adjusted, say, once AI-based facial recognition is ubiquitous, perhaps with laws specific to certain applications of technology.

The prospect exists of more disruptive risks, such as a malevolent or indifferent AI, but they are not unmanageable. There has been no historical shortage of malevolent or indifferent human rulers. While it is exceptionally unlikely that people will destroy the world for the sake of paperclips, they could destroy it for other reasons. The purpose of the law and our systems of checks and balances is, in part, to constrain bad behavior and manage risk, whether from an unscrupulous policy maker or a James Bond–style techno-villain. Society may be exchanging one set of risks for another with AI, but the risks are not necessarily worse or less susceptible to management. The possibility of harm does not mean we should not embrace activities, or new technologies, where the benefits will likely outweigh the costs. And, while there are plenty of legitimate risks with AI, there is no reason to think that AI able to act intelligently will have self-awareness and be driven by a desire for self-preservation.

CONCLUDING THOUGHTS

Artificial intelligence may be the most disruptive and inventive technology ever created, but it is not guaranteed to improve lives. The way to ensure it does is through enacting appropriate laws and policies for AI. Policymakers should be concerned with the functionality of machines and consequentialist benefits – what will result in the greatest social benefit from these technologies – in deciding how to legally treat AI. At the end of the day, people do not concern themselves with whether a self-driving Tesla with an unpredictable neural network, a self-driving Uber using Good Old-Fashioned AI, or a human driver is behind the wheel of a car coming toward them. They – we – simply do not want to be run over.

Of the many principles relevant for regulation, it is important to include the principle of AI legal neutrality to ensure that unnecessary barriers are not erected that prevent us from realizing the benefits of AI. Artificial intelligence is not part of our moral community, but it needs to be part of our legal one to promote human welfare. In time, as AI increasingly outperforms people at exercising judgment and eventually becomes the accepted way in which we solve problems, AI should replace us in our legal standards. The ancient Greek philosopher Protagoras claims that "man is the measure of all things." As AI increasingly steps into the shoes of people, it should become the measure of all things. Our challenge then may be less about how to regulate AI and more about how to regulate ourselves.

Third-Party Materials

Some material in this book was adapted from the author's prior works, including two coauthored works, reprinted with permission.

- Ryan Abbott, *I Think, Therefore I Invent: Creative Computers and the Future of Patent Law*, 57 BOSTON COLLEGE LAW REVIEW 1079 (2016).
- Ryan Abbott, *The Reasonable Computer: Disrupting the Paradigm of Tort Liability*, 86 THE GEORGE WASHINGTON LAW REVIEW 1 (2018).
- Ryan Abbott and Bret Bogenschneider, *Should Robots Pay Taxes? Tax Policy in the Age of Automation*, 12 HARVARD LAW & POLICY REVIEW 145 (2018).
- Ryan Abbott, *Everything Is Obvious*, 66 UCLA LAW REVIEW 1 (2019).
- Ryan Abbott and Alexander Sarch, *Punishing Artificial Intelligence: Legal Fiction or Science Fiction*, 53 UC DAVIS LAW REVIEW 323 (2019).

Notes

INTRODUCTION: ARTIFICIAL INTELLIGENCE AND THE LAW

1. Kazimierz O. Wrzeszczynski et al., *Comparing Sequencing Assays and Human-Machine Analyses in Actionable Genomics for Glioblastoma*, 3 NEUROL. GENET. (2017), DOI: 10.1212/NXG.000000000000164.
2. Eliza Strickland, *How IBM Watson Overpromised and Underdelivered on AI Health Care*, IEEE SPECTRUM, Apr. 2, 2019, https://spectrum.ieee.org/biomedical/diagnostics/how-ibm-watson-overpromised-and-underdelivered-on-ai-health-care.
3. BENJAMIN NATHAN CARDOZO, SELECTED WRITINGS OF BENJAMIN NATHAN CARDOZO 417 (Margaret E. Hall ed., 1947).
4. ORGANISATION FOR ECONOMIC CO-OPERATION AND DEVELOPMENT, PRINCIPLES ON ARTIFICIAL INTELLIGENCE (2019), www.oecd.org/going-digital/ai/principles/.
5. MINISTRY OF FOREIGN AFFAIRS OF JAPAN, G20 MINISTERIAL STATEMENT ON TRADE AND DIGITAL ECONOMY (2019), www.mofa.go.jp/files/000486596.pdf.
6. Matt Krantz, *PepsiCo Paid No Tax? Neither Did These Other 33 Profitable S&P 500 Companies*, INVESTOR'S BUSINESS DAILY, July 18, 2019, www.investors.com/etfs-and-funds/personal-finance/corporate-tax-rate-zero-profitable-us-companies-sp500/.
7. Richard Rubin, *Does Amazon Really Pay No Taxes? Here's the Complicated Answer*, THE WALL STREET JOURNAL, June 14, 2019, www.wsj.com/articles/does-amazon-really-pay-no-taxes-heres-the-complicated-answer-11560504602.
8. GEAR 2030, FINAL REPORT OF THE HIGH-LEVEL GROUP ON THE COMPETITIVENESS AND SUSTAINABLE GROWTH OF THE AUTOMOTIVE INDUSTRY IN THE EUROPEAN UNION, at 40 (July 2017).
9. Timothy B. Lee, *Autopilot Was Active When a Tesla Crashed into a Truck, Killing Driver*, ARS TECHNICA, May 16, 2019, https://arstechnica.com/cars/2019/05/feds-autopilot-was-active-during-deadly-march-tesla-crash/?comments=1&post=37374819.
10. Beat Weibel, *AI Created Inventions – Digital Inventor Computer-Implemented Simulations – Digital Twin*, WIPO CONVERSATION ON INTELLECTUAL PROPERTY (IP) AND ARTIFICIAL INTELLIGENCE (AI), Sept. 30, 2019, www.wipo.int/meetings/en/doc_details.jsp?doc_id=454861.
11. *Ex parte* Stephen L. Thaler, No. BL O/741/19 (U.K. I.P.O. Dec. 4, 2019).
12. See www.artificialinventor.com for the current status of these applications.
13. Law No. 071, Ley de Derechos de la Madre Tierra, Diciembre 21, 2010, LA ASAMBLEA LEGISLATIVA PLURINACIONAL (Bolivia), www.planificacion.gob.bo/uploads/marco-legal

/Ley%20N%C2%B0%20071%20DERECHOS%20DE%20LA%20MADRE%20TIERRA
.pdf.
14. Emails with Arno Nickel, InfinityChess General Manager (Nov. 7 & 10, 2019) (on file
    with author).

1 UNDERSTANDING ARTIFICIAL INTELLIGENCE

1. HOMER, THE ILIAD OF HOMER (Richmond Lattimore trans., University of Chicago Press
   1951).
2. Isaac Asimov, *Runaround, in* I, ROBOT 40 (Isaac Asimov Collection ed., Doubleday 1950).
3. J. McCarthy, M. L. Minsky, N. Rochester, & C. E. Shannon, A *Proposal for the
   Dartmouth Summer Research Project on Artificial Intelligence*, Aug. 31, 1955, www
   .formal.stanford.edu/jmc/history/dartmouth/dartmouth.html.
4. Andrew Griffin, *"Russia's Most Modern Robot" Revealed to Be Just a Person in a Suit*, THE
   INDEPENDENT, Dec. 12, 2018, www.independent.co.uk/life-style/gadgets-and-tech/news/
   russia-robot-person-in-suit-fake-hoax-most-modern-advanced-a8680271.html.
5. STUART RUSSELL & PETER NORVIG, ARTIFICIAL INTELLIGENCE: A MODERN APPROACH (3rd ed.
   2009).
6. Shane Legg & Marcus Hutter, *Universal Intelligence: A Definition of Machine
   Intelligence*, 17 MINDS AND MACHINES 391, 444 (2007).
7. René Descartes, *Discourse on Method, in* 1 THE PHILOSOPHICAL WRITINGS OF DESCARTES
   109, 109–151 (John Cottingham, Robert Stoothoff, & Dugald Murdoch trans., Cambridge
   University Press 1985).
8. *Id.* at Part V.
9. Irving J. Good, *Speculations Concerning the First Ultraintelligent Machine, in* ADVANCES
   IN COMPUTERS 33, 31–87 (Ser. No. 6, 1965).
10. Vincent C. Müller & Nick Bostrom, *Future Progress in Artificial Intelligence: A Survey of
    Expert Opinion, in* FUNDAMENTAL ISSUES OF ARTIFICIAL INTELLIGENCE 553, 553–571
    (Vincent C. Müller ed., 2016).
11. *See* JAMES BARRAT, OUR FINAL INVENTION: ARTIFICIAL INTELLIGENCE AND THE END OF THE
    HUMAN ERA 152 (2013).
12. Alan M. Turing, *Computing Machinery and Intelligence*, 59 MIND 433, 433 (1950).
13. HERBERT A. SIMON, MODELS OF MY LIFE (MIT Press 1996).
14. Quoc V. Le et al., *Building High-Level Features Using Large Scale Unsupervised
    Learning, in* INTERNATIONAL CONFERENCE IN MACHINE LEARNING 507 (2012).
15. Alex Kizhevsky, Ilya Sutskever, & Geoffrey E. Hinton, *ImageNet Classification with Deep
    Convolutional Neural Networks*, 60 COMMUNICATIONS OF THE ACM 84 (2017).
16. EUROPEAN COMMISSION PRESS RELEASE IP/18/3362, ARTIFICIAL INTELLIGENCE: COMMISSION
    OUTLINES A EUROPEAN APPROACH TO BOOST INVESTMENT AND SET ETHICAL GUIDELINES,
    Apr. 25, 2018, https://europa.eu/rapid/press-release_IP-18-3362_en.htm.
17. Ophir Tanz, *Can Artificial Intelligence Identify Better than Humans?*, ENTREPRENEUR,
    Apr. 1, 2017, www.entrepreneur.com/article/283990.
18. Dave Gershgorn, *The Quartz Guide to Artificial Intelligence: What Is It, Why Is It
    Important, and Should We Be Afraid?*, QUARTZ, Sept. 10, 2017, https://qz.com/1046350/
    the-quartz-guide-to-artificial-intelligence-what-is-it-why-is-it-important-and-should-we-
    be-afraid/.
19. Rory Smith, *The Google Translate World Cup*, THE NEW YORK TIMES, July 13, 2018, www
    .nytimes.com/2018/07/13/sports/world-cup/google-translate-app.html.

20. Wendy Hall & Jérôme Pesenti, *Growing the Artificial Intelligence Industry in the UK*, Oct. 2017, https://assets.publishing.service.gov.uk/government/uploads/system/uploads/attach ment_data/file/652097/Growing_the_artificial_intelligence_industry_in_the_UK.pdf.

21. PRICEWATERHOUSECOOPERS, *Sizing the Prize: What's the Real Value of AI for Your Business and How Can You Capitalise?* (2017), www.pwc.com/gx/en/issues/analytics/ assets/pwc-ai-analysis-sizing-the-prize-report.pdf.

22. Richard Dobbs, James Manyika, & Jonathan Woetzel, *The Four Global Forces Breaking All the Trends*, MCKINSEY GLOBAL INSTITUTE (2015), www.mckinsey.com /business-functions/strategy-and-corporate-finance/our-insights/the-four-global-forces -breaking-all-the-trends.

23. James Vincent, *Twitter Taught Microsoft's AI Chatbot to Be a Racist Asshole in Less Than a Day*, THE VERGE, Mar. 24, 2016, www.theverge.com/2016/3/24/11297050/tay-microsoft-chatbot-racist.

24. Peter Bright, *Tay, the Neo-Nazi Millennial Chatbot, Gets Autopsied*, ARS TECHNICA, Mar. 25, 2016, https://arstechnica.com/information-technology/2016/03/tay-the-neo-nazi-millennial-chatbot-gets-autopsied.

2 SHOULD ARTIFICIAL INTELLIGENCE PAY TAXES?

1. Ryan Abbott & Bret Bogenschneider, *Should Robots Pay Taxes? Tax Policy in the Age of Automation*, 12 HARV. L. & POL'Y REV. 145, 145–175 (2018).

2. THOMAS MORTIMER, LECTURES ON THE ELEMENTS OF COMMERCE, POLITICS AND FINANCES 72 (A. Straham, for T. N. Longman and O. Rees 1801).

3. DAVID RICARDO, ON THE PRINCIPLES OF POLITICAL ECONOMY AND TAXATION 283–84 (Batoche Books 2001) (3rd ed. 1821).

4. THOMAS CARLYLE, THE WORKS OF THOMAS CARLYLE: CRITICAL AND MISCELLANEOUS ESSAYS 141–142 (Henry Duff Trail ed., Cambridge University Press 2010) (1899).

5. JAGDISH BHAGWATI, ALAN S. BLINDER, & DOUGLAS A. IRWIN, OFFSHORING OF AMERICAN JOBS 80 (The MIT Press 2009).

6. JOHN STUART MILL, PRINCIPLES OF POLITICAL ECONOMY 97 (Cosimo Classics 2006) (1848).

7. Carl Benedikt Frey & Michael A. Osborne, *The Future of Employment: How Susceptible Are Jobs to Computerisation?*, 114 TECH. FORECASTING & SOCIAL CHANGE 254 (2013), www .oxfordmartin.ox.ac.uk/downloads/academic/The_Future_of_Employment.pdf.

8. OXFORD ECONOMICS, HOW ROBOTS CHANGE THE WORLD (2019), www .oxfordeconomics.com/recent-releases/how-robots-change-the-world.

9. Forrester, The Future of Work (2019), https://go.forrester.com/future-of-work/? utm_source=forrester_news&utm_medium=web&utm_campaign=futureofwork.

10. BANK OF AMERICA, ROBOT REVOLUTION – GLOBAL ROBOT & AI PRIMER 3 (Dec. 16, 2015).

11. James Manyika et al., *Jobs Lost, Jobs Gained: What the Future of Work Will Mean for Jobs, Skills, and Wages*, McKinsey Global Institute (2017), www.mckinsey.com/fea tured-insights/future-of-work/jobs-lost-jobs-gained-what-the-future-of-work-will-mean -for-jobs-skills-and-wages#part3.

12. Akshat Rathi, *Stephen Hawking: Robots Aren't Just Taking Our Jobs, They're Making Society More Unequal*, QUARTZ, Oct. 9, 2015, http://qz.com/520907/stephen-hawking -robots-arent-just-taking-our-jobs-theyre-making-society-more-unequal/.

13. Klaus Schwab & Richard Samans, PREFACE TO WORLD ECON. F., THE FUTURE OF JOBS: EMPLOYMENT, SKILLS AND WORKFORCE STRATEGY FOR THE FOURTH INDUSTRIAL REVOLUTION, at v–vi (2016), www3.weforum.org/docs/WEF_Future_of_Jobs.pdf.

14. John Stuart Mill, Principles of Political Economy with Some of Their Application to Social Philosophy (Longmans, Green, and Co. 1909) at Book I, ch. VI, ¶ 13.
15. Exec. Office of the President, Comm. on Tech., & Nat'l Sci. & Tech. Council, Preparing for the Future of Artificial Intelligence 2 (2016), https://obamawhitehouse .archives.gov/sites/default/files/whitehouse_files/microsites/ostp/NSTC/preparing_ for_the_future_of_ai.pdf.
16. Aria Bendix, *One of the World's Largest Basic-Income Trials, a 2-Year Program in Finland, Was a Major Flop. But Experts Says the Test Was Flawed*, Business Insider (2019), www.businessinsider.com/finland-basic-income-experiment-reasons-for-failure -2019-12.
17. Exec. Office of the President, Artificial Intelligence, Automation, and the Economy 3 (2016), https://obamawhitehouse.archives.gov/sites/whitehouse.gov/files/documents/ Artificial-Intelligence-Automation-Economy.PDF.
18. James Manyika et al., *A Future That Works: Automation, Employment, and Productivity*, McKinsey Global Institute (2017), at 21, www.mckinsey.com/~/media/mckinsey/fea tured%20insights/Digital%20Disruption/Harnessing%20automation%20for%20a% 20future%20that%20works/MGI-A-future-that-works-Executive-summary.ashx.
19. Bret N. Bogenschneider, The Tax Paradox of Capital Investment, 33 J. Tax'n Inv. 59, 74 (2015).
20. *See, e.g.,* Katia Dmitrieva & Laura Davison, *Corporate America Is Repatriating a Fraction of Foreign Profits*, Bloomberg, June 20, 2019, www.bloomberg.com//amp// news//articles//2019-06-20//corporate-america-is-repatriating-a-fraction-of-foreign-profits (referring to President Donald Trump's estimate that US businesses would repatriate $4 trillion in offshore cash holdings as a result of the 2017 tax law).
21. Internal Revenue Serv., U.S. Dep't of the Treasury, Pub. 970, SOI Tax stats – collections and refunds, by Type of Tax – IRS Data Book Table 1 (2019), https://www.irs.gov/statistics/ soi-tax-stats-collections-and-refunds-by-type-of-tax-irs-data-book-table-1.
22. *See* Lester Snyder & Marianne Gallegos, *Redefining the Role of the Federal Income Tax: Taking the Tax Law "Private" Through the Flat Tax and Other Consumption Taxes*, 13 Am. J. Tax Pol'y 86 (1996).
23. Internal Revenue Serv., U.S. Dep't of the Treasury, Pub. 970, Student Loan Interest Deduction 31 (2019), www.irs.gov/pub/irs-pdf/p970.pdf.
24. Bret N. Bogenschneider, A *Theory of Small Business Tax Neutrality*, 15 FSU Bus. Rev. 33 (2016); *see also* Bret N. Bogenschneider, *The European Commission's Idea of Small Business Tax Neutrality*, 25 EC Tax Rev. 221 (2016).
25. Stuart Adam, Tax by Design 41 (Oxford University Press 2011), www.ifs.org.uk\\uploads\ \mirrleesreview\\design\\ch2.pdf.

3 REASONABLE ROBOTS

1. *Improvements in Workplace Safety – United States, 1900–1999*, 48 CDC Morbidity & Mortality Wkly. Rep. 461, 461 (1999). The National Safety Council estimates that 18,000–21,000 workers died from work-related injuries in 1912. *Id.*
2. Bureau of Labor Statistics, U.S. Dep't of Labor, National Census of Fatal Occupational Injuries in 2017, at 1 (2018), http://www.bls.gov/news.release/pdf/cfoi.pdf.
3. Oliver Wendell Holmes Jr., *The Theory of Torts*, 7 Am. L. Rev. 652, 653 (1873) *in* 1 The Collected Works of Justice Holmes 327 (Sheldon M. Novick ed., 1995).
4. *Gardiner* v. *Gray* (1815) 171 Eng. Rep. 46, 47 (K.B.).

5. *Id.* at 1054.

6. Erin Stepp, *Three-Quarters of Americans "Afraid" to Ride in Self-Driving Vehicle*, AAA NEWSROOM, Mar. 1, 2016, http://newsroom.aaa.com/2016/03/three-quarters-of-americans-afraid-to-ride-in-a-self-driving-vehicle/.

7. David Neal, *Over Half of Brits Won't Feel Safe Using the Streets with Driverless Cars*, THE INQUIRER, Oct. 17, 2016, www.theinquirer.net/inquirer/news/2474351/over-half-of-brits-wont-feel-safe-using-the-streets-with-driverless-cars.

8. Michele Bertoncello & Dominik Wee, *Ten Ways Autonomous Driving Could Redefine the Automotive World*, MCKINSEY & CO., June 2015, www.mckinsey.com/industries/automotive-and-assembly/our-insights/ten-ways-autonomous-driving-could-redefine-the-automotive-world.

9. Martin A. Makary & Michael Daniel, *Medical Error – The Third Leading Cause of Death in the US*, 353 BMJ 2139, 2139 (2016); *See also* INST. OF MED., TO ERR IS HUMAN: BUILDING A SAFER HEALTH SYSTEM (Linda T. Kohn et al., eds., 2000).

10. *See* SAE INT'L, AUTOMATED DRIVING (2014), http://www.sae.org/misc/pdfs/automated_driving.pdf (describing the SAE taxonomy).

11. OLIVER WENDELL HOLMES JR., THE COMMON LAW, 108 (1881).

12. Roberts v. Ring, 143 Minn. 151, 153 (1919).

4 ARTIFICIAL INVENTORS

1. Ryan Abbott, *The Artificial Inventor Project*, WIPO MAGAZINE, Dec. 2019, www.wipo.int/wipo_magazine/en/2019/06/article_0002.html.

2. Leo Kelion, *AI System "Should Be Recognized as Inventor,"* BBC, Aug. 1, 2019, www.bbc.co.uk/news/technology-49191645.

3. *See What Is the Ultimate Idea?*, IMAGINATION ENGINES INC., www.imagination-engines.com.

4. *See* U.S. Patent No. 5,852,815 (filed May 15, 1998).

5. *See* Tina Hesman, *Stephen Thaler's Computer Creativity Machine Simulates the Human Brain*, ST. LOUIS POST-DISPATCH, Jan. 24, 2004, www.mindfully.org/Technology/2004/Creativity-Machine-Thaler24jan04.htm (quoting Rusty Miller).

6. Jonathon Keats, *John Koza Has Built an Invention Machine*, POPULAR SCI., Apr. 18, 2006, https://popsci.com/scitech/article/2006-04/john-koza-has-built-invention-machine/.

7. *Id.*

8. U.S. Patent No. 6,847,851 (filed July 12, 2002).

9. Telephone Interview with John Koza, President, Genetic Programming Inc. (Jan. 22, 2016) (on file with author).

10. *See* John R. Koza, *Human-Competitive Results Produced by Genetic Programming*, 11 GENETIC PROGRAMMING & EVOLVABLE MACHINES 251, 265 (2010).

11. Douglas B. Lenat & William R. Sutherland, *Heuristic Search for New Microcircuit Structures: An Application of Artificial Intelligence*, 3 AI MAG., 17, 17 (1982).

12. U.S. provisional patent application SN 144,960 (filed Apr. 29, 1980). Email communications with Katherine Ku, Dir. of Stanford Office of Tech. Licensing, to author (Jan. 17, 2018) (on file with author).

13. Alexander Kott, *Artificial Invention: Synthesis of Innovative Thermal Networks, Power Cycles, Process Flowsheets and Other Systems*, ii (Dissertation.com, 2005), www.bookpump.com/dps/pdf-b/1122640b.pdf.

14. *See Computational Creativity*, IBM, https://perma.cc/6FK4-WTL3.

15. *What Is Watson?*, IBM, https://perma.cc/8KM3-LLSG.
16. *See Computational Creativity, supra* note 14.
17. 35 U.S.C. § 101 (1952).
18. Anne Gulland, *Scientists Claim to Have Developed World's First Vaccine with Artificial Intelligence,* THE TELEGRAPH, July 3, 2019, www.telegraph.co.uk/global-health/science -and-disease/scientists-claim-have-developed-worlds-first-vaccine-artificial/.
19. 35 U.S.C. § 154.
20. Townsend v. Smith, 36 F.2d 292, 295 (C.C.P.A. 1929).
21. *Id.*
22. Beat Weibel, *AI Created Inventions – Digital Inventor Computer-Implemented Simulations – Digital Twin,* WIPO CONVERSATION ON INTELLECTUAL PROPERTY (IP) AND ARTIFICIAL INTELLIGENCE (AI), Sept. 30, 2019, www.wipo.int/meetings/en/doc_details.jsp? doc_id=454861.
23. U.S. CONST. art. I, § 8, cl. 8.
24. Heli Pihlajamaa, *Legal Aspects of Patenting Inventions Involving Artificial Intelligence (AI): Summary of Feedback by EPC Contracting States,* COMMITTEE ON PATENT LAW, Feb. 20, 2019, http://documents.epo.org/projects/babylon/eponet.nsf/0/3918F57B010A3540C125841900280 653/$File/AI_inventorship_summary_of_answers_en.pdf.
25. U.S. COPYRIGHT OFFICE, COMPENDIUM OF U.S. COPYRIGHT OFFICE PRACTICES (FIRST) § 2.8.3 (1st ed. 1973).
26. Martin L. Klein, *Syncopation in Automation,* RADIO-ELECTRONICS, June 1957, at 36.
27. U.S. COPYRIGHT OFFICE, COMPENDIUM OF U.S. COPYRIGHT OFFICE PRACTICES § 313.2 (3d ed. 2014).
28. In re Trade-Mark Cases, 100 U.S. 82, 94 (1879).
29. *See* Burrow-Giles Lithographic Co. v. Sarony, 111 U.S. 53, 56 (1884).
30. NAT'L COMM'N ON NEW TECH., USES OF COPYRIGHTED WORKS, FINAL REPORT ON NEW TECHNOLOGICAL USES OF COPYRIGHTED WORKS 1 (1979).
31. *Id.* at 45.
32. Arthur R. Miller, *Copyright Protection for Computer Programs, Databases, and Computer-Generated Works: Is Anything New Since CONTU?,* 106 HARV. L. REV. 977, 1070 (1993).
33. Naruto v. David John Slater et al., No. 16-15469 (9th Cir. 2018).
34. Copyright, Designs and Patents Act, 1988 § 178.
35. Copyright, Designs and Patents Act, 1988 § 9(3).
36. Express Newspapers plc v. Liverpool Daily Post & Echo [1985] FSR 306.
37. *Id.*
38. Whitford Committee on Copyright Designs and Performers Protection (Cmnd 6732 HMSO 1977), para 514.
39. Nova Productions Ltd v. Mazooma Games Ltd [2006] EWHC 24.
40. Nova Productions Ltd v. Mazooma Games Ltd [2006] EWHC 24 [106].
41. Keats, *supra* note 6.
42. Cuno Engineering Corp. v. Automatic Devices Corp., 314 U.S. 84, 91 (1941).
43. Graham v. John Deere Co. of Kan. City, 383 U.S. 1, 15 n. 7, 16 n. 8 (1966).
44. *The "Flash of Genius" Standard of Patentable Invention,* 13 FORDHAM L. REV. 84, 87 (1944).
45. Jungersen v. Ostby & Barton Co., 335 U.S. 560, 572 (1949) (Jackson, J., dissenting).
46. *The "Flash of Genius" Standard of Patentable Invention, supra* note 44, at 85 (internal quotation marks omitted).
47. *See* William N. Eskridge Jr. & Phillip P. Frickey, *Statutory Interpretation as Practical Reasoning,* 42 STAN. L. REV. 321, 340 (1989–1990).

48. Diamond v. Chakrabarty, 447 U.S. 303, 315 (1980).
49. Ken Jennings, *My Puny Human Brain*, SLATE, Feb. 16, 2011, http://primary.slate.com /articles/arts/culturebox/2011/02/my_puny_human_brain.html.
50. Diamond v. Chakrabarty, 447 U.S. at 308 (quoting 5 WRITINGS OF THOMAS JEFFERSON 75–76 (H. Washington ed. 1871)). "In choosing such expansive terms [for the language of Section 101] ... modified by the comprehensive 'any,' Congress plainly contemplated that the patent laws would be given wide scope . . . ." *Id.*

5 EVERYTHING IS OBVIOUS

1. VI WRITINGS OF THOMAS JEFFERSON, LETTER TO ISAAC MCPHERSON (Washington ed. 1813) [hereinafter LETTER TO ISAAC MCPHERSON], at 180–181.
2. Hotchkiss v. Greenwood, 52 *U.S.* (11 How.) 248, 267 (1850).
3. *Id.*
4. McClain v. Ortmayer, 141 *U.S.* 419, 427 (1891).
5. Gay Chin, *The Statutory Standard of Invention: Section 103 of the 1952 Patent Act*, 3 PAT. TRADEMARK & COPY. J. RES. & ED. 317, 318 (1959).
6. Cuno Engineering Corp. v. Automatic Devices Corp., 314 U.S. 84, 84 (1941).
7. CLS Bank Int'l v. Alice Corp. Pty. Ltd., 717 F.3d 1269, 1295 (Fed. Cir. 2013).
8. 35 U.S.C. § 103 (2006).
9. Uniroyal Inc. v. Rudkin-Wiley Corp., 837 F.2d 1044, 1050, 5 U.S.P.Q. (BNA) 1434, 1438 (Fed. Cir. 1988).
10. KSR International Co. v. Teleflex Inc., 550 U.S. 398, 418 (2007).
11. Standard Oil Co. v. American Cyanamid Co., 774 F.2d 448, 454 (Fed. Cir. 1985).
12. In re Bigio, 381 F.3d 1320, 1325 (Fed. Cir. 2004).
13. In re Winslow, 365 F.2d 1017, 1020 (C.C.P.A. 1966).
14. Merit Mfg. Co. v. Hero Mfg. Co., 185 F.2d 350 (2d Cir. 1950).
15. In 1966, in *Graham*, the Supreme Court recognized that "the ambit of applicable art in given fields of science has widened by disciplines unheard of a half century ago. ... [T]hose persons granted the benefit of a patent monopoly [must] be charged with an awareness of these changed conditions." Graham v. John Deere Co., 383 U.S. 1, 19 (1966).
16. Kimberly-Clark Corp. v. Johnson & Johnson, 745 F.2d 1437, 1454 (Fed. Cir. 1984).
17. Mobil Oil Corp. v. Amoco Chems. Corp., 779 F. Supp. 1429, 1442–1443 (D. Del. 1991).
18. *Id.*
19. Gregory Mandel, *The Non-Obvious Problem: How the Indeterminate Nonobviousness Standard Produces Excessive Patent Grants*, 42 U. C. DAVIS, L. REV. 57, 64 (2008).
20. Graham, 383 U.S. at 11.
21. KSR Int'l Co., *supra* note 10 at 402.
22. James M. Buchanan & Yong J. Yoon, *Symmetric Tragedies: Commons and Anticommons*, 43 J. L. & COM. 1, 2 (2000).
23. KSR Int'l Co., *supra* note 10 at 398.

6 PUNISHING ARTIFICIAL INTELLIGENCE

1. Gabriel Hallevy, *The Criminal Liability of Artificial Intelligence Entities: The Criminal Liability of Artificial Intelligence Entities – From Science Fiction to Legal Social Control*, 4 AKRON INTELLECTUAL PROPERTY JOURNAL 171, 191 (2010).
2. *Id.* at 199.

3. *Id.* at 201.

4. *Id.* at 199.

5. Ying Hu, *Robot Criminals*, 52 MICHIGAN J. L. REFORM 487, 531 (2019).

6. H.L.A. HART, PUNISHMENT AND RESPONSIBILITY 4–5 (2nd ed., 2008).

7. Peter Asaro, *A Body to Kick, but Still No Soul to Damn: Legal Perspectives on Robotics, in* ROBOT ETHICS: THE ETHICAL AND SOCIAL IMPLICATIONS OF ROBOTICS 181 (2011).

8. Mark A. Lemley & Bryan Casey, *Remedies for Robots* (Stanford Law and Economics Olin Working Paper No. 523, 2018), http://dx.doi.org/10.2139/ssrn.3223621.

9. Christina Mulligan, *Revenge Against Robots*, 69 S. CAROLINA. L. REV. 579, 580 (2018); *cf.* David Lewis, *The Punishment that Leaves Something to Chance*, 18 PHIL. & PUB. AFF. 53, 54 (1989).

10. Mulligan, *supra* note 9 at 593.

11. ANTONY DUFF, THE REALM OF THE CRIMINAL LAW 19 (2018).

12. *Id.*

13. Model Penal Code, § 2.01(1).

14. Gideon Yaffe, *The Voluntary Act Requirement, in* THE ROUTLEDGE COMPANION TO THE PHILOSOPHY OF LAW 174 (Andrei Marmor ed., 2012).

15. Michael Bratman, INTENTION, PLANS AND PRACTICAL REASON 141–142 (1999). *See also* Alex Sarch, *Double Effect and the Criminal Law*, 11 CRIM. L. AND PHILOS. 453, 467–468 (2015).

16. Bratman, *supra* note 15 at 141.

17. Hart at 4.

18. Elizabeth Harman, *Harming as Causing Harm, in* HARMING FUTURE PERSONS 139 (Melinda A. Roberts and David T. Wasserman eds., 2009).

19. PHILIPPA FOOT, NATURAL GOODNESS 26 (2001) ("features of plants and animals have what one might call an 'autonomous', 'intrinsic', or as I shall say 'natural' goodness and defect that may have nothing to do with the needs or wants of the members of any other species of living thing").

20. Joel Feinberg, *The Rights of Animals and Unborn Generations, in* PHILOSOPHY AND ENVIRONMENTAL CRISIS 43, 49–52 (William T. Blackstone ed., 1974).

21. Mulligan, *supra* note 9 at 594.

22. EUR. PARL. DOC. (A8-0005/2017), http://www.europarl.europa.eu/sides/getDoc.do?pubRef=-//EP//TEXT+REPORT+A8-2017-0005+0+DOC+XML+V0//EN.

23. Open Letter to the European Commission Artificial Intelligence and Robotics (Apr. 5, 2018), https://g8fip1kplyr33r3krz5b97d1-wpengine.netdna-ssl.com/wp-content/uploads/2018/04/RoboticsOpenLetter.pdf.

24. Luisa Damiano & Paul Dumouchel, *Anthropomorphism in Human–Robot Co-evolution*, FRONT. PSYCHOL., Mar. 26, 2018, https://doi.org/10.3389/fpsyg.2018.00468.

25. Lewis, *supra* note 9 at 54.

26. Kate Darling, *Extending Legal Protection to Social Robots: The Effects of Anthropomorphism, Empathy, and Violent Behavior Towards Robotic Objects, in* ROBOT LAW 213, 215 (Ryan Calo, A. Michael Froomkin, & Ian Kerr eds., 2016).

27. Citizens United v. Fed. Election Comm'n, 558 U.S. 310, 341 (2010) and Burwell v. Hobby Lobby Stores Inc., 573 U.S. 682 (2014).

28. Terrorism Act 2006 (UK), § 5, www.legislation.gov.uk/ukpga/2006/11/introduction.

7 ALTERNATIVE PERSPECTIVES ON AI LEGAL NEUTRALITY

1. TU WEIMING, CONFUCIAN THOUGHT: SELFHOOD AS CREATIVE TRANSFORMATION (Albany: State University of New York Press, 1985).

2. AI HIGH LEVEL EXPERT GROUP (HLEG), EUROPEAN COMMISSION, ETHICS GUIDELINES FOR TRUSTWORTHY ARTIFICIAL INTELLIGENCE (Apr. 8, 2019), https://ec.europa.eu/digital-single-market/en/news/ethics-guidelines-trustworthy-ai.

3. See Julia Angwin, Jeff Larson, Surya Mattu, & Lauren Kirchner, *Machine Bias*, PROPUBLICA (May 23, 2016), www.propublica.org/article/machine-bias-riskassessments-in-criminal-sentencing.

4. France Bans Judge Analytics, 5 Years In Prison for Rule Breakers, ARTIFICIAL LAWYER (June 4, 2019), www.artificiallawyer.com/2019/06/04/france-bans-judge-analytics-5-years-in-prison-for-rule-breakers/.

5. *See, e.g.,* Jaya Ramji-Nogales, Andrew Schoenholtz, & Philip G. Schrag, *Refugee Roulette: Disparities in Asylum Adjudication*, 60 STAN. L. REV. 295 (2008).

6. Andrew Dansby, *Country Scribe Harlan Howard Dies*, ROLLING STONE (Mar. 5, 2002), www.rollingstone.com/music/music-news/country-scribe-harlan-howard-dies-197596/.

7. Casey Chan, *Is It Mathematically Possible to Run Out of New Music*, GIZMODO (Nov. 20, 2012), https://gizmodo.com/is-it-mathematically-possible-to-run-out-of-new-music-5962375.

8. *See, e.g.,* Nicholas J Hudson, *Musical Beauty and Information Compression: Complex to the Ear but Simple to the Mind?*, 4 BMC RESEARCH NOTES 9 (2011).

9. Kenneth Anderson & Matthew C. Waxman, *Debating Autonomous Weapon Systems, Their Ethics, and Their Regulation Under International Law, in* THE OXFORD HANDBOOK OF LAW, REGULATION, AND TECHNOLOGY (Roger Brownsword, Eloise Scotford, & Karen Yeung, eds. 2017). Available at SSRN: https://ssrn.com/abstract=2978359.

10. Eric Niiler, *Can AI Be a Fair Judge in Court? Estonia Thinks So*, WIRED (Mar. 25, 2019), www.wired.com/story/can-ai-be-fair-judge-court-estonia-thinks-so/.

11. F.E.A. Sander & S.B. Goldberg, *Fitting the Forum to the Fuss: A User-Friendly Guide to Selecting an ADR Procedure*, 10 NEGOTIATION JOURNAL 49–67 (1994).

12. Nick Bostrom, *Ethical Issues in Advanced Artificial Intelligence, in* 2 COGNITIVE, EMOTIVE AND ETHICAL ASPECTS OF DECISION MAKING IN HUMANS AND IN ARTIFICIAL INTELLIGENCE 12–17 (I. Smit et al. eds., 2003).

Index

CPSIA information can be obtained
at www.ICGtesting.com
Printed in the USA
LVHW020557040922
727497LV00016B/676

9 781108 459020